Inside the Vatican of Pius XII

Inside the
Vatican of Pius XII

The Memoir of an American Diplomat
During World War II

Harold H. Tittmann, Jr.

EDITED BY

Harold H. Tittmann III

Image Books
Doubleday

New York London Toronto Sydney Auckland

AN IMAGE BOOK
PUBLISHED BY DOUBLEDAY
a division of Random House, Inc.

Book design by Fearn Cutler de Vicq

Library of Congress Cataloging-in-Publication Data
Tittmann, Harold H., 1893–1980.
Inside the Vatican of Pius XII : the memoir of an American diplomat during World War II /
edited by Harold H. Tittmann, III.
p. cm.
1. Pius XII, Pope, 1876–1958. 2. World War, 1939–1945—Catholic Church. 3. Europe—
Politics and government—1918–1945. I. Tittmann, Harold H. II. Title.
BX1378.T58 2003
327.730456'34'09044—dc22   2003062903

ISBN 0-385-51129-9

July 2004
Image Books
First Edition
1 2 3 4 5 6 7 8 9 10

Contents

Acknowledgments

Editing these memoirs would have been far more difficult and time consuming had it not been for the remarkable work performed by Lucy Tittmann, my sister-in-law, in organizing my father's manuscript and related papers. She devoted much time during my father's last years, as well as after his death, to this task, thus greatly facilitating the production of this book.

My brother Barclay has been most helpful in proposing improvements to my text, as well as in supplementing and correcting my recollections of our Vatican sojourn.

I am also grateful to Father Peter Gumpel, S.J., of the Jesuit Order headquarters in Rome, for his careful review of the manuscript of this book and correcting a few factual errors.

Finally, a word of thanks to Jo Esterhazy, who was my secretary many years ago, for efficiently transcribing my father's manuscript onto my computer.

Introduction

*H*arold H. Tittmann, Jr., my father, served thirty-eight years in
the U.S. Foreign Service, rising to the highest rank of Career
Ambassador, a remarkable feat for a man who lost a leg and suffered
other severe wounds in World War I. He was of course proud of his
ambassadorships, but considered the two and a half years he spent
inside the Vatican City as Chargé d'Affaires of the United States during World War II to be the high point of his career. This unprecedented assignment and its evident historical interest inspired him to
write these memoirs, the story of a unique episode in the annals of
U.S. diplomacy.

The Tittmann family originated from the Saxon city of Dresden.
My father's grandfather emigrated to the United States in the middle
of the nineteenth century, settling in St. Louis, Missouri, where my
father was born in 1893. He graduated from Yale University in
1916, and after a year in business, he enlisted in the U.S. Army Air
Service when the United States entered World War I. In June 1918,
he was assigned to Eddie Rickenbacker's famous 94th ("Hat in the
Ring") Pursuit Squadron, based at Toul, in northeastern France. On
July 3 of that year, while on patrol over German-held territory, he
was attacked by five German fighter planes, one of which he probably shot down. Although severely wounded, he was able to fly back
to the French lines and crash-land in a wheat field.

At the U.S. military field hospital where he was taken, his condi-

*tion was considered hopeless, but endowed with a strong will to sur-
vive, he nevertheless recovered, losing his right leg, a kidney and half
of one lung, incurring as well major bone damage to his arms and
remaining leg. He spent nearly two years in Army hospitals, and was
reputed to be the most severely wounded-in-action American to have
survived in the First World War. He was awarded the U.S. Distinguished Service Cross for Extraordinary Heroism, as well as the
French Croix de Guerre.*

*In 1920, my father joined the U.S. Foreign Service and was
assigned to the American embassy in Paris as Third Secretary. In
1925, he was posted to the Rome embassy, where he remained for the
next eleven years, thus becoming one of the State Department's leading experts on Fascist Italy. There he met Eleanor Barclay, from San
Antonio, Texas; they were married in 1928. I was born in 1929 and
my brother Barclay followed in 1932.*

*In 1936, my father was transferred to the State Department in
Washington, spending three years in the Division of Western European Affairs. In August 1939, a few weeks prior to the outbreak of
World War II, he was assigned to Geneva, Switzerland, as Consul
General. His involvement with the Vatican began in February of the
following year, when, in addition to his Geneva post, he served as
part-time assistant to Myron Taylor, President Roosevelt's newly
appointed personal representative to Pope Pius XII. At the end of
1940, he was transferred to Rome as Counselor at the U.S. Embassy,
where the State Department, in view of the tense situation between
the United States and Italy, believed his experience could best be put
to use. Shortly thereafter, he was permanently attached to Myron
Taylor's Vatican mission, spending two and a half years inside Vatican City with his family following Italy's declaration of war on the
United States in December 1941. After Rome was liberated in 1944,
he moved back there, where he remained as assistant to Myron Taylor until 1946, when he was appointed Ambassador to Haiti. In*

1948, he was named Ambassador to Peru, a post he held until 1955. After three years as Director of the Intergovernmental Committee for European Migration in Geneva, he retired in 1958 and moved to Washington, D.C.

In retirement, my father devoted himself to writing the memoirs of his Vatican assignment, covering the period from August 1939 to June 1944, when Rome was liberated and our family moved out of the Vatican. In putting together this book, I have adhered to the original text of my father's writings except where I felt they needed editing to improve their readability. I have not, however, modified in any way his opinions and recollections. His narrative is well organized and generally complete up to the end of 1943. But the manuscripts covering the first half of 1944 were unfinished, and consequently, they had to be extensively edited and reorganized. In doing so, I have relied primarily on my father's main sources, name-ly the State Department's Foreign Relations of the United States *and the Vatican's* Actes et Documents *of the Second World War. He preserved many of his wartime letters to his family and other per-sons, which have also been helpful in completing the narrative.*

My father's narrative appears in this book in roman type; the italic print represents my contributions, consisting primarily of a commen-tary providing background information and filling in the occasional gaps in my father's narrative. In addition, I have included some child-hood memories of the Swiss and Vatican wartime period, based in part on a diary I kept, as well as my brother Barclay's recollections.

My father died in Manchester, Massachusetts, on December 29, 1980, a few days prior to his eighty-eighth birthday.

Inside the Vatican of Pius XII

CHAPTER I

1939–1940

*I*n August 1939, my father was appointed U.S. Consul General
in Geneva, Switzerland. At that time, Hitler was threatening
to invade Poland if the Poles did not meet his demands regarding
Danzig and the Polish Corridor. Despite British and French com-
mitments to support Poland if the Germans attacked, Europeans did
not want to believe that the Polish crisis would lead to yet another
major war. Nevertheless, World War II broke out shortly after my
father began his new assignment in Geneva, and he recorded his
impressions of this dramatic event in his memoirs:

A week before the Nazis invaded Poland, I arrived in Geneva to
assume my new job as Consul General. It was the end of August
in 1939. I had come from Washington where I had been in the
Division of Western European Affairs at the State Department.
Looking back, it seems extraordinary that, although we knew
many of the details regarding efforts to keep the peace, we
somehow lacked awareness that Europe was on the brink of a
real disaster. My family was with me; after docking at Le Havre,
we motored through France, stopping on the way to enjoy the
countryside and to leave our ten year old son, Harold, with
American friends outside of Paris for a visit. But he surprised us
by arriving in Geneva on the train only one day after we ourselves arrived, explaining as he got off the train that his hosts

had suddenly departed for the United States, convinced that France was about to go to war. During our brief stay in France we had not been conscious of the imminence of such danger, and the French people we talked with did not seem at all disturbed. Even when I arrived at my office in Geneva, I encountered little sense of impending danger. Our son had first brought us the sad tidings.

It was at a bathing beach in Geneva on September 3, with family and friends, that we heard over the loudspeaker the British and French prime ministers announce to the world that their countries were at war with Germany. There was practically no reaction. We all simply shrugged our shoulders and continued to enjoy the warm autumn sun and the refreshing water of the lake. This extraordinary display of apathy in the light of such catastrophic forebodings was an example of the sentiment that prevailed everywhere in Europe during the following six months. Only Switzerland immediately put in strict rationing. After the surrender of Poland, military activities on both sides were at a standstill and neither one displayed any desire to get them started. This was called the period of the "phony war."

When we first arrived in Geneva, we stayed at Hotel de la Paix for a month or so while my parents looked for a house to rent. The hotel, relatively small and cozy, was one of Geneva's best, located on a lakeside quai only two blocks from the offices of the Consulate General. I remember particularly the elegant dining room, which had a superb view of the lake and Geneva's trademark jet d'eau, a graceful artificial geyser thrusting hundreds of feet above the lake. One day at lunch, my father commented to the headwaiter that it obviously must be expensive to provide enough energy to throw up so much water. Wouldn't it be better for mankind, my father added, if the

funds spent for this spectacle were used instead to help the poor?
"Monsieur," replied the headwaiter, "there are no poor people in
Switzerland." Indeed, there were no slums in Geneva; the city dis-
played subdued, well-ordered prosperity that the wartime restric-
tions would not seriously affect.

We soon moved to "Campagne Mallet," a lovely seventeenth-
century country house rented by my father in the Geneva suburb of
Cologny. I remember particularly the extensive grounds surrounding
the house, which included a working farm where we obtained fresh
eggs. Campagne Mallet provided my father, for the only time in his
career, with an opportunity to create a small vegetable garden, despite
his wooden leg. He managed to grow a few rows of American sweet
corn, which matured nicely in the summer of 1940. The driveway
leading to the villa was lined by two rows of magnificent horse chest-
nut trees, which in the fall produced an abundant crop of shiny
brown fruit. Though inedible for humans, they were used by the
Swiss farmers as emergency wartime rations for their pigs. My broth-
er Barclay and I would collect the horse chestnuts in large sacks,
which we were able to sell for a modest amount of pocket money.

My parents chose to continue our schooling at least partly in the
English language. Although Barclay and I had learned to speak
French at an early age from Swiss governesses in Rome, our writing
ability was nil. After a brief stint at the International School in
Geneva, my father sent me to Le Rosey, a fashionable boarding
school for boys located halfway between Geneva and Lausanne. The
school was bilingual in French and English, and was known for
attracting the sons of royalty and the wealthy from all over the
world. After the war broke out, the school's sources of students large-
ly dried up, allowing my father to negotiate a reduced tuition, the
normal size of which he could ill afford. During the winter term, the
entire school would move to a campus in the ski resort of Gstaad. I
have only vague recollections of that school year, my first away from

home, but I think on the whole it was a happy time and I received a good education. Although the number of students had shrunk from 110 to around 30, the school kept on all its faculty. As a result, the students benefited from unusually close attention from the teachers.

As the "phony" war continued into 1940, my father found his work in Geneva "much too quiet for [his] taste," as he wrote to his mother in February 1940. One of the functions of the Consulate General in Geneva was to report on developments at the League of Nations, which was based in that city. However, the League was in its death throes, and not much of interest was happening. My parents were warmly received by Geneva society; my father speculated that this was partly due to self-interest, as the Swiss may have foreseen the day when they would need the wartime support of the United States. This does not do justice to the great charm and social graces of my mother. She was an accomplished golfer, and soon became the ladies' champion at the Geneva Golf Club.

At the end of 1939, President Roosevelt decided to appoint Myron C. Taylor as his personal representative to Pope Pius XII. It was a decision that would have a profound effect on my father's diplomatic career. His memoirs describe the background to the Taylor mission:

In November 1936, Eugenio Cardinal Pacelli, the Secretary of State of Pius XI, was the luncheon guest of President Roosevelt at his country estate at Hyde Park, and the question of relations between the U.S. and the Vatican was broached in a general way. Thereafter, Roosevelt often referred to Pacelli, especially after he became Pope Pius XII, as "his old and good friend," a personal and familiar touch which was unusual when statesmen dealt with the Pope. Although there was no formal change in the traditional policy of United States aloofness from Vatican affairs, Roosevelt demonstrated a more sympathetic attitude toward the Pope and the Holy See by designating Joseph

Kennedy, the U.S. Ambassador in London, as Special Envoy of the President at the Coronation Ceremony of Pacelli as the newly elected Pope on March 12, 1939. This was the first time an American president had been officially represented on such an occasion.

During the summer of 1939, as the war clouds were gathering and turning black, President Roosevelt became convinced of the need for establishing some rapport with the Holy See, in view of its importance in world affairs. The Vatican had representatives, diplomatic or otherwise, in a total of seventy-two countries throughout the world, from which it could gather much information. In addition, the diplomatic corps accredited to the Holy See, representing thirty-eight countries, constituted in itself a potential source of useful information.

In July 1939, Under Secretary of State Sumner Welles sent a personal letter to William Phillips, the U.S. Ambassador in Rome, asking for his thoughts on the possible establishment of U.S.–Vatican diplomatic relations. Phillips replied that he favored such a move, since this would make available to the Department of State an important source of political information. Phillips also noted that U.S. diplomatic relations with the Vatican would enhance the prestige of the Pope and thus help him in his dealings with the Italian and German governments, as well as in his efforts to preserve the peace in Europe. "At present," Phillips wrote, "the Pope is living in the shadow of a dominant personality and he may well hesitate at times to take any action that might incur the displeasure of Mussolini."

In August, Welles and Secretary of State Cordell Hull advised Roosevelt that the Vatican had many sources of information, particularly for Germany, Italy and Spain, which the U.S. did not possess, and that it was obviously desirable to obtain access to such information. Hull recommended against the appointment of a regular ambassador, which would require the consent of the Senate. Instead, he suggested the naming of a personal representative of the President to the Pope, thereby avoiding Senate involvement. The Vatican had for years maintained an informal "Apostolic Delegation" in Washington, which had no diplomatic standing.

In October, Archbishop Spellman of New York, who had close contacts with the Pope, met with Roosevelt to discuss relations with the Vatican. The President told him that he had decided to establish a special U.S. mission to the Holy See which would not require Congressional approval. In order to make sure that there would be no interference by the Congress, he planned to announce the decision during the Christmas legislative recess. He advised Spellman that his representative would be either Myron C. Taylor, ex-Chairman of U.S. Steel Corporation, or Breckinridge Long, a former ambassador to Italy and currently an Assistant Secretary of State—both Protestants. After informing the Vatican of his conversation with the President, Spellman advised Roosevelt that either candidate would be entirely acceptable to the Holy Father.

In a Christmas message to the Pope, Roosevelt informed him of his decision to appoint a personal representative, Myron Taylor, who would carry the rank of ambassador, but without the formal title. In a letter of confirmation to Taylor, Roosevelt requested him to proceed to the Vatican as soon as possible to act as a channel of communication between the Pope and himself and to report to Washington on "any matters which may come to your attention in the performance of your mission and which you feel may serve the best interests of the United States." Taylor, aged sixty-six, was a close friend of Roosevelt, a leading U.S. business executive and a wealthy man. He also served as the President's representative on the Inter-Governmental Committee on Political Refugees, established in 1938 to facilitate the emigration to the Western Hemisphere of refugees, many of them Jewish, from Germany and German-occupied territories.

The establishment of the Taylor mission soon met with strenuous objections from Protestant quarters, who viewed it as a violation of the constitutional separation of church and state. Conscious of this non-Catholic opposition in the U.S., the President attempted to disassociate as much as possible the Taylor mission in the eyes of the public from a formal diplomatic appointment. Mr. Taylor would constantly emphasize the unusual and unofficial aspects of his position, letting it be known that all his reports were addressed directly to the President outside official government channels. This was not exactly the case, since such reports only rarely escaped the notice of the Secretary of State or even the ambassador to Italy, the American Embassy being the only safe means of communication between Taylor and Roosevelt. Moreover, Taylor served without salary from the government, and his expenses were paid from funds appropriated from the Inter-Governmental Committee on Refugees.

Roosevelt's first objective in sending Taylor to the Vatican was to join forces with the Pope in attempting to persuade Mussolini to keep Italy out of the war. Roosevelt was determined to assist the British and French in their struggle against Nazi Germany in every possible way, and maintaining Italy's nonbelligerent status was a key element of the President's strategy. He knew that the Pope, fearing that Italy's entry into the war, in addition to the inevitable human suffering, would result in massive damage to the Catholic Church's incomparable religious and artistic assets in Italy, was pursuing the same goal.

Roosevelt requested the State Department to provide logistical support to Taylor, and in early February my father, because of his intimate knowledge of Italy, was ordered to join Taylor in Rome as

his "assistant." *The assignment was temporary, as my father continued to hold the post of Consul General in Geneva. He did not have
great expectations about his new job; he wrote to his mother that he
had been "ordered to proceed to Rome to act as a cicerone to Mr.
Myron Taylor . . . I have not the least idea what I am expected to do."
But he looked forward to returning to Italy.*

*My father traveled to Rome on February 20, 1940, establishing
his quarters in the Excelsior Hotel on the Via Veneto. A few days
later, Myron Taylor arrived from the United States. Taylor was an
imposing person, the archetype of the successful big business executive, in both appearance and personality. He was a man clearly used
to commanding; one Italian official, who visited Taylor in Florence
when he was ill in bed, felt that, despite his prone position, he
appeared to be sitting on a throne.*

*Taylor also settled in the Excelsior; his large suite would serve as
the base for his mission. For the next six weeks, my father accompanied Taylor on a constant round of official calls on Vatican officials
and on diplomats accredited to the Holy See. Taylor would then
receive return calls from these dignitaries at the Excelsior. As Easter
approached, the Vatican diplomatic corps attended a series of religious
services. My father recalled one particularly dramatic ceremony:*

Towards evening on the Thursday before Easter of that porten-
tous year 1940, the office of the Matins of Tenebrae began in
Santa Maria Maggiore in Rome as the clergy silently entered the
magnificent basilica, now dark and bare. The only light, coming
from the small number of wax tapers distributed around the
high altar, flickered dimly on the paneled ceiling above, which
had been covered centuries ago with gold from the New World.
The lovely melodious "Miserere," the gradual extinction of the
candles one by one and afterwards the praying in complete dark-

ness and silence when not even a bell was heard, and finally the resounding noise echoing down the ancient aisles produced by the beating on benches with iron bars to recall the disturbance of the forces of nature at the approach of Christ's death, were all intensely dramatic. As we were leaving the basilica, Ambassador Taylor turned to me and grimly reflected that the noise caused by the beating on the wood could also represent the ferment then pervading Europe, the ominous developments of 1939 and 1940.

My father had little to do with Taylor's dealings with the Pope and did not attend his numerous papal audiences. Taylor had brought along his personal secretary, and prepared his reports to President Roosevelt on these meetings with the Pope entirely on his own. Moreover, during the crucial months of April, May, and June, my father spent only one week in Rome with Taylor. His memoirs consequently describe the diplomatic aspects of the Taylor mission essentially in terms of an outside observer:

On the western side of the Atlantic, there was deep concern over the situation in Europe. President Roosevelt did not shut his eyes to the fast-deteriorating political situation; in fact he had been watching developments very closely. According to Italian archives seized by the Germans when they occupied Rome in 1943 and later recaptured and publicized by the Allies, the President played an increasingly important role in the various attempts to keep Italy neutral since the end of 1939. These files reveal that on January 6, 1940, he proposed to the Italians a "common, effective action" by the Pope, Mussolini, and himself "for the restoration of peace in Europe," and had even expressed the desire for a personal conference with the Duce sometime in 1940.

Not surprisingly, Myron Taylor's appointment and the public exchange of messages between the Pope and the President, created the image of a triumvirate composed of Pius XII, Roosevelt, and Mussolini combining to bring about a peace that would be 1) anti-Bolshevist as proposed by the Holy See, 2) pro-capitalist as desired by the United States and 3) providing a European balance-of-power according to Italian concepts. In a meeting at the White House during the latter part of January with the Italian Ambassador in Washington, Don Ascanio dei Principi Colonna, President Roosevelt requested the envoy to convey to Mussolini his ardent desire that Italy should continue to remain a nonbelligerent, as she had declared when war erupted.

Then on February 26, 1940, Under Secretary of State Sumner Welles, in Rome for the first of two visits to the Italian capital during a fact-finding tour in Europe, met the Duce and delivered a letter from President Roosevelt in which the oral request already made through Ambassador Colonna was repeated in writing. The Pope assured Myron Taylor and Sumner Welles, at an audience on March 18, that Roosevelt could perform a valuable service in the interest of peace by exerting his influence on the Duce to keep Italy out of war.

Mr. Taylor was granted private audiences with the Holy Father on seven different occasions during this critical period in 1940—February 27, the Pope's birthday, March 2 with Sumner Welles present, March 18, March 29, April 26, May 11 and May 23—an unusually large number of audiences accorded to any one foreign diplomat over so short a period. The main theme of the conversations between the two was the necessity for devising without delay some means to keep Mussolini out of the war. Both admitted as events proceeded that there was little hope that their endeavors could meet with success. From the beginning the Pope kept stressing the fact that President Roosevelt's influence on Mussolini would be of key importance and the Cardinal Secretary of State, Maglione, on his part informed Mr.

Taylor that Roosevelt's authority in world affairs could be more powerful than that of any single statesman or group of statesmen in the West.

The British Government itself was willing to go to great lengths to keep Italy out of the war. On April 18, a message from the British Foreign Secretary, Lord Halifax, to Myron Taylor, delivered by the British Minister to the Holy See, D'Arcy Osborne, stated:

> Please tell Mr Taylor that this is undoubtedly a critical moment and I should be very grateful for anything he could advise the President to do with a view to restraining Mussolini of the feeling he is believed to entertain that the Allies' aim is destroying the Fascist Regime in Italy as well as the Nazi Regime in Germany. It would, therefore, be helpful if Mr Taylor would suggest to the President that he might impress upon high circles in Italy the fact that we are in friendly relations with many countries which are governed by an authoritarian regime and that the kind of regime prevailing in other countries is no business of ours.

Lord Halifax then pointed out that the British Government had never thought of placing the Nazis of Hitler and the Fascists of Mussolini on the same plane and ended his message by saying that while he understood that the Duce might be convinced that Germany was invincible, he nevertheless felt that Mussolini should realize that he could have much greater influence in the reconstruction of Europe if he were to stay out of the melee altogether.

On April 19, Taylor telegraphed to President Roosevelt that he had conferred with the Cardinal Secretary of State, the

British minister and the French, Belgian, Romanian, Polish and Spanish ambassadors to the Holy See and, of course, with the American ambassador to Italy, William Phillips, as well. They all agreed that the situation of Italy vis-à-vis Germany was uncertain and critical and that there was a real danger of Mussolini either joining Hitler or engaging separately in new aggressions. They expressed belief that an immediate communication from the President to Mussolini urging that he refrain from this type of action would be most desirable. Taylor asked Cardinal Maglione whether the Pope would be prepared to take "parallel action" with the President for peace by also appealing to the Duce. Maglione replied that he would need to consult with the Pope before giving an answer. Taylor advised the President:

> I am definitely convinced that a communication from you to Mussolini would be timely and helpful and can be so worded as to contain no possibility of harmful results either to our own country, considering our neutral position, or to yourself. In any event, it seems to me that this is the only remaining effort you can make at this moment to try to circumscribe the war.

The next day, on April 20, 1940, the Pope sent word to Taylor that he agreed with him completely and that he should urge President Roosevelt, in the name of the Holy Father, to make an immediate personal appeal to the Duce to keep Italy out of the war and that the Vatican would take the "parallel action" suggested at the same time. The Pope warned, however, that because of the necessity to preserve the neutral status of the Holy See, Vatican participation in such a combined effort should not be revealed. On April 26, the Pope addressed a handwritten letter to Mussolini urging him to remain neutral.

President Roosevelt's initial reaction to Mr. Taylor's telegram was negative. He had already sent two similar appeals to the Duce, which he felt should be sufficient. The State Department therefore informed Taylor on April 25 that, while the President himself did not believe the moment opportune for another Presidential message, he nevertheless saw no reason why the Holy Father, if he saw fit, should not make his own independent approach to Mussolini. Taylor cabled to Washington the next day that he had again been to see the Pope as well as the Cardinal Secretary of State to inform them of Washington's negative attitude. Although disappointed, they were convinced more than ever, as Mr. Taylor was himself, that the President should repeat his appeals without delay.

In his reply dated April 30 to the Pope's handwritten letter, the Duce appreciated the Holy Father's recognition of his own tireless efforts to avoid the war which broke out in September. He then declared that if it had not been for the "absurd" Franco-British precondition insisting upon the return beforehand of the German armed forces already on the move in Poland back to their line of departure in Germany, the peace conference he had in mind for the first days of September could have taken place and not only the Polish problem would have been solved, but also other questions that were awaiting settlement. He concluded by stating that he could give the Pope no absolute assurance that Italy would not enter the war, since everything depended on the attitudes of third parties (not identified), but he could promise that Italy would not take part in the conflict unless her honor, interests and her future absolutely demanded it.

In the meantime, President Roosevelt experienced a change of heart and decided after all to take the requested action. No doubt this was not due alone to the exhortations of the Pope and Mr. Taylor, but also to the further entreaties of British, French and other statesmen who had now become desperate as a result of the mounting German military successes. President Roosevelt's action took the form of a message read personally on May 1 to Mussolini by Ambassador Phillips. The "parallel action" to persuade Mussolini to refrain from entering the war was thus being implemented.

To President Roosevelt's communication, the Duce answered that peace was not possible until the fundamental problems of Italian liberty had been settled (which might mean anything). The reply from Mussolini was read to the President at the White House on May 2 by the Italian Ambassador in Washington and the President took the opportunity afforded by the meeting to request the Ambassador once again to convey urgently to the Duce the desire of the United States that Italy should not enter the war. This was the President's fourth appeal.

In spite of the two unsatisfactory responses from the Duce, Mr. Taylor, at the insistence of the Pope, continued to beg the President to continue his efforts to influence Mussolini in the right direction and to keep the current contacts alive. The reaction in the White House this time was favorable, and three more Presidential messages went forward in rapid succession to Mussolini on May 14, May 27 and May 31, delivered through the Italian Foreign Minister since the Duce had bluntly refused to receive Ambassador Phillips personally.

Mr. Taylor had become so discouraged by the hopelessness of the outlook that he had sent a telegram on May 17 to President Roosevelt suggesting that he be ordered to return to Washington for consultation. He felt that there was no further reason for continuing the "parallel action" with the Holy Father which was the main purpose for his presence in Rome. However, the President instructed Mr. Taylor to remain at his post in view of the fluidity of the situation. In spite of the Duce's negative or noncommittal replies to the urgent appeals of the American President (seven in five months), certain quarters in Washington felt that, with the situation becoming more critical by the hour, still another attempt should be made to sway the Fascist leader. Accordingly, an eighth message from the President to Mussolini was actually drafted in the State Department on June 7. By this time, no doubt, loud cries of "enough!" could be heard in the White House, with the result that this final project was dropped.

On May 10, the German Army invaded Belgium and the Nether-lands, and the relative calm reigning at the Geneva Consulate General was shattered. The State Department, fearing that the Germans would soon attack France through Switzerland as well, ordered my father to arrange for the repatriation to the United States of consular staff families. He obeyed with reluctance, as the move was most unpopular with the families concerned, who did not appreciate the inconveniences, particularly the interruption of the school year for children. Viewed from Geneva, the State Department's fears seemed exaggerated, as there were no indications that the Germans intended to test the resistance of the well-equipped and -trained Swiss Army.

The Tittmann family was of course included in the repatriation program. I was instructed by the headmaster of Le Rosey to pack my suitcase and join my mother and brother in Geneva. The next day, along with several other consular families, the three of us boarded a train for Paris, and spent the next two days at the Hotel Crillon. Since the German advance was threatening to cut off the usual route back to the United States, via Le Havre and the United Kingdom, the American Embassy in Paris recommended that we head for Por-tugal, where we could eventually board a Pan American flying boat linking Lisbon to the United States. The Embassy advised us to make a stopover in southwestern France and await developments at the front, where the French and British armies were still resisting.

We settled in a hotel in the Basque seaside resort of St. Jean de Luz. It was hard to realize that there was a war on, except for the growing flow of refugees from northern France and Belgium passing through on their way to Spain and Portugal. The hotel was comfortable and the food plentiful and excellent. By the middle of June it became evident that France was defeated, and my mother decided that it was time to move on to Portugal. The first step was to go by car to the Spanish city of San Sebastian, which was only a short distance from St. Jean de Luz. But it took us many hours to cross the Spanish frontier because of the flood of refugees fleeing from the approaching German Army. At the Spanish border, our car happened to be next to a magnificent Mercedes convertible, loaded with luggage and a supply of French baguettes. A distinguished-looking lady sat in the back seat: she was the Grand Duchess of Luxembourg, who was also fleeing the Germans.

We spent the next night in San Sebastian. The contrast between France, even during wartime, and Spain was striking. The city looked drab, the hotel not very comfortable, and the food dismal— all of which was not surprising, since the Spanish Civil War had only just ended. The next day we boarded a train for Lisbon, where we stayed in a hotel in the seaside resort of Estoril. The comforts of life in Portugal were a great improvement over Spain, and we spent several weeks enjoying the delightful beaches of the Portuguese Riviera, awaiting our turn to board the flight back to the United States.

By this time, France had capitulated, the Pétain government establishing itself in Vichy, controlling an area in central and southeastern France unoccupied by German troops. Switzerland had not been invaded by the Germans, and it was now clear that its neutrality would not be violated. My father decided that it was no longer necessary for us to return to the United States, and we happily agreed. We flew to Barcelona on an Italian airliner to meet my father, who had motored from Geneva to pick us up. My father recorded in a letter to a friend in the United States that the trip to Geneva through unoccupied France was uneventful, except for frequent identity controls by the French military. Thousands of unarmed French soldiers loitered by the roadsides, waiting to be discharged. The French populace seemed to be accepting the defeat of their nation with stoicism, relieved that the dreadful butchery of the First World War had not repeated itself. Food was plentiful and good. Our family saga as privileged "war refugees" ended when we arrived in Geneva on July 10. In the meantime, the Taylor mission to the Vatican was winding down, having failed to achieve its aim of keeping Italy out of the conflict.

At 6 P.M. on Monday, June 10, Mussolini announced to the Italian people that on the following day Italy would be at war with Great Britain and France. He spoke from his famous balcony overlooking Piazza Venezia in Rome before a large crowd, which demonstrated less enthusiasm than usual.

Before the war, when Rome had become the seat of the Fascist government headed by a dictator who had never felt warmly toward the Holy See, Vatican officials had been clearly unhappy. After Italy became a belligerent, they were gripped by anxiety almost amounting to despair. When rumors circulated that the Fascist Black Shirt militia were about to force their way into the Vatican to seize its archives, the Holy See was inclined to believe them. It requested the Italian Government to adopt appropriate measures "to prevent the dignity and independence of the Holy See, so solemnly guaranteed by the Lateran Accords, from being assailed." On June 14, the Italian Government assured the Vatican that there was no foundation to the rumors, but Vatican officials feared that under war conditions, Mussolini would be more inclined than ever to ignore the Lateran Accords and impose his will on the Pope. The Duce could do this by simply cutting off vital supplies such as water, gas, and electricity.

The Vatican had to tackle the immediate problem of the status of diplomats accredited to the Holy See representing countries now at war with Italy. In peacetime, all diplomatic missions to the Vatican were located in Rome, in accordance with the Lateran Treaty. Article 12 of that treaty was supposed to cover the case of diplomats from belligerent countries, but the wording of the provision was admittedly vague. It did not make an explicit reference to war condtions, but stated that foreign envoys could continue to remain on Italian territory, "even though their countries might not maintain diplomatic relations with Italy." In discussions with the Italian Government which had taken place from time to time since 1938, when it became likely that Italy might become a belligerent, the Vatican had always insisted that under the Treaty, the diplomats of enemy countries should be able to continue to exercise their functions in Rome. However, the Italian Government kept evading the issue. In May 1940, the question became acute and embarrassing for the Vatican, but it was only towards the end of that month that the Italian Government made clear its position. The Italian Foreign Minister, Count Ciano, informed the Apostolic Nuncio to Italy that diplomatic representatives to the Holy See of countries that might eventually be at war with Italy would have to leave Italian soil and establish their residences within the neutral state of the Vatican City.

When Italy went to war, the Holy See had no choice but to offer the affected diplomats these alternatives:

1. They could return to their home countries or move to a neutral country in Europe, where they could keep in touch with the Vatican through its diplomatic representatives, or

2. Following the suggestion of the Italian Government, they could accept the Pope's invitation to move into the

Vatican, there to remain interned for the duration of the war as his guests.

The representatives of Great Britain, France, Belgium, and Poland were instructed by their governments to remain near the Pope, come what may. The Holy Father was pleased to act as host to the Allied diplomats, and living quarters were made available to all four missions in the Hospice of Santa Marta, located in the southwest corner of Vatican City and reached by turning sharp left after entering the Vatican from St. Peter's Square through the Gate of the Bells. Santa Marta served in peacetime as a hostel for pilgrims from abroad, but upon arrival of the diplomats, it was turned into a form of "compound." Because of its high walls, iron gate and guard house, Vatican gendarmes could easily keep track of the movements of the diplomats, which by request of the Italian government were reported to the Italian police.

The gated entrance to Santa Marta opened onto a spacious courtyard adorned by a large statue of the Virgin and Child overlooking a fountain carpeted by white-flowered Madonna lilies. On the right was the five-story main building, the "palazzo," with enough space to accomodate the four diplomatic missions. Across the courtyard stood a two-floor annex, the "palazzino," which later would also be used to house diplomats. The Sisters of the Order of St. Vincent de Paul, in their steel-blue habits and wide-winged white coifs, administered Santa Marta and operated a refectory on the ground floor of the main building for Santa Marta residents who did not take their meals in their lodgings. The apartments assigned to the diplomats were modest, having previously served as dormitories for pilgrims, but they were comfortable and clean.

Thus, within a matter of days following Italy's entry into the war, the envoys of the four Allied nations were safely ensconced with their staffs and families inside the Vatican, where, with the exception of the Belgians, they were destined to reside for the next four years until the liberation of Rome by the Allied armies. Ciano reportedly favored this solution, as he could imagine circumstances arising in the future when it would be useful for him to contact enemy countries through their representatives in the Vatican.

The Belgian Ambassador, Adrien Nieuwenhuys, moved into the Vatican even though Italy had not formally declared war on his country. However, a few months later, he appealed through the Vatican to the Italian authorities to allow him to return to his embassy residence in Rome because of ill health. He was suffering from neurasthenia, which manifested itself through a continuing fear that he would eventually be punished for not supporting his King, Leopold III, after the latter had surrendered to the German Army in Belgium. Nieuwenhuys was afraid that the King might consider him a deserter for joining the Allied diplomats in the Vatican. Furthermore the incessant ringing of the bells of St. Peter's aggravated his condition. The Italian Government eventually granted Nieuwenhuys permission to return to his Rome residence, after ascertaining that King Leopold bore no grudge of any kind against him. The Pope himself was glad to have an ambassador return to his Rome residence, as it showed that the Italians were respecting the provisions of the Lateran Treaty. On the other hand, Nieuwenhuys's colleagues who remained in the Vatican were unhappy, because they felt that his position as an Allied sympathizer had been compromised by the acceptance of a favor from the Fascist Government. As time went on, Nieuwenhuys proved to be an ardent supporter of the Allied cause.

On June 15, Taylor fell seriously ill with gall-bladder trouble and ten days later was operated on in the presence of an American doctor and a trained nurse whom Mrs. Taylor had brought with her from New York especially for the occasion. The operation was successful. He then planned to leave for New York on August 23. The failure of the "parallel action" of the Holy Father and President Roosevelt to keep Italy out of the war came as a severe blow to each of them and, of course, to Myron Taylor as well, who now felt more than ever that his usefulness in Rome had come to an end. Shortly before his departure, the Holy Father granted an audience to Taylor, who found the Pope in a depressed state of mind. The British, Italian, and German governments had reacted negatively to his confidential peace enquiries of June 28, when he had asked the three governments to study the possibility of an agreement to end the war. Their coolness made it plain that there was not the slightest hope for the success of such a project.

A further Vatican peace effort later in July had also been rebuffed by the British. On July 19, speaking once more from the Reichstag, the German Chancellor addressed a direct appeal to Great Britain for an immediate cessation of hostilities. Lord Halifax bluntly turned this down. On July 25, the American Ambassador to Belgium, John Cudahy, who happened to be traveling through Rome on the way to the United States, was received by the Holy Father. The American diplomat was obviously concerned with Britain's plight and was convinced that the British were in no position to resist a German invasion. Cudahy therefore believed that the acceptance by England of peace negotiations with Germany would be preferable to an invasion. He suggested to the Pope that it was the right moment for the Pontiff to take another step toward peace by advising the British government, perhaps this time through Cardinal Hinsley, Archbishop of Westminster, to avoid giving the impression to the world that it had completely rejected Hitler's offer. Regardless of its worth, Cudahy believed that the British should at least request the German government to specify in detail its ideas for peace.

Pope Pius XII took Ambassador Cudahy's recommendation to heart and the next day instructed the Apostolic Delegate in London, Monsignor Godfrey, to get in touch with Cardinal Hinsley, in order to discuss the matter with him and possibly to approach the British government itself. The reply from the Delegate on July 29 indicated that both he and the Cardinal agreed that the Pope's suggestion, if presented to the British government, could easily be misinterpreted as associating the Holy See with Hitler's efforts to persuade Great Britain to accept the present situation without further fighting. Furthermore, the Delegate reported that the British government did not in any way regard the German Chancellor's Reichstag speech as a peace offer. Cardinal Hinsley observed that the Hitler Reichstag speech was a tissue of insults and threats.

The British Minister to the Holy See, D'Arcy Osborne, was much less intransigent than either Cardinal Hinsley or Monsignor Godfrey. When the Secretary of State, Cardinal Maglione, who was embarrassed by the reports from London, permitted Osborne to read the exchange of communications between the Vatican and London, the British Minister stated that he had fully approved of the Pope's initiative because he had understood the spirit with which it was taken and was not pleased with the unyielding attitudes of the two British ecclesiastics. He felt, as did Ambassador Cudahy, that Great Britain should avoid giving the impression to the world that she had abandoned every possibility for peace and should embrace any honorable opportunity that presented itself in the future. He also said that he understood perfectly that there was no idea in the

Pope's mind of pressing England to capitulate or of humiliating that country. Osborne promised Maglione that he would advise the Foreign Office in London immediately of his own personal feelings in the matter, but the attitude of the British Government remained unchanged.

The Pope's attempts to bring about peace had all failed. He had tried to prevent the war from breaking out; when it did he tried to stop it; and then in 1940 he tried to keep Italy neutral. The only thing left for him now was to dedicate himself to the humanization of the now irrevocable ordeal. The Holy Father told Myron Taylor during their final audience that he was especially concerned over the future of Great Britain, which seemed very black indeed. When Taylor endeavored to comfort him with visions of the vast potential of American military and economic aid, the Pope replied that, although he was impressed by Taylor's words, he feared that the aid would turn out to be too little and too late.

I left Geneva on August 17 and made my third and last trip to Italy, this time to bid farewell to Mr. Taylor. Because of his uncertain health, he was unable to set a firm date for his next visit to Rome. I was instructed to return to my post in Geneva, and thus the Roosevelt mission at the Vatican became inactive. I had been in Italy for only sixty-six days in 1940. In the United States, however, Mr. Taylor continued to remain in close touch with the Holy See through the Apostolic Delegation in Washington.

For the remainder of 1940, my father remained at his post as Consul General in Geneva. "Geneva is now a most interesting place," he wrote to his mother on August 22, "the crossroads of all travel in Europe today. We have had a constant stream of diplomats and ordinary Americans from the northern European countries, all with stories one taller than the other—except that the stories are true." But in December, he was permanently assigned to Rome.

CHAPTER 2

1941

*I*941 *turned out to be a complicated year for my parents. As a result of my father's transfer to Rome at the end of 1940, my mother had to run our large villa, Campagne Mallet, entirely on her own under difficult wartime conditions. Since my brother and I were in the middle of our school year at the Ecole Communale de Cologny, moving to Rome was out of the question. My parents hired a young Swiss woman, Jane Morerod, as governess, permitting my mother to spend a few months in Rome. The thought of moving his family to an Italy at war did not appeal to my father, since the risk of air raids was always present. Fortunately for my parents, Rome and Geneva were only an overnight train trip apart. Despite the war, the Wagons Lits service remained comfortable and efficient in 1941; the British bombing campaign against Italy had not yet seriously affected it.*

On December 5, 1940, I received word in Geneva that I was to be transferred to Rome as Counselor of the United States Embassy. At the end of the month I arrived in the Italian capital ready to assume my new duties, but this time I returned to Rome with a heavy heart. During my several tours of duty at the Vatican mission earlier in the year, I had become convinced that, considering Mussolini's increasing reserve, verging on hostility, towards everything American, there was no longer any chance for effective action for peace through American diplomacy. In view of the Roman environment of official cynicism and contempt towards efforts to improve relations, I believed that American interests would have been better served if the State Department had allowed me to remain in Switzerland where there was at least some freedom of action and where there was a friendly atmosphere in which to work. Also, Geneva had become a mine of all types of information.

However, my superiors in Washington, seemingly impressed by my experience in Italy, understandably felt that if ever there was a time or place in which I could be of some service to my country as a diplomat, it was at that moment in Rome. The sensation of helplessness on my part was intensified by the uncertainty of the fate in store for my wife and two sons who were still in Switzerland, a neutral country surrounded on all sides by war and devastation. The decision soon had to be made whether they should return to the United States while it was still possible to do so, or whether by electing to remain near me, risk another hegira more hazardous than their first experience as refugees.

Upon my arrival in Rome, I moved once again into the Excelsior Hotel on the Via Veneto, close to the offices of our Embassy. I chose a hotel, rather than a house or apartment, because the location was especially convenient for my work, and also because it hardly seemed worthwhile to burden myself with housekeeping now that wartime rationing of food, fuel and other items was becoming more severe by the day. Furthermore, it was impossible to make plans for my family to come to Rome for any length of time. The plenitude of work at the Embassy helped mitigate the general atmosphere of pessimism. In addition to our routine duties, we, as an embassy of a country still nominally at peace, had taken over the local interests of ten different countries, including Great Britain and the Commonwealth countries, France, Belgium, Norway, Luxembourg, and Egypt.

My immediate superior and Chief of the Embassy staff was Alexander Kirk, a career officer and Chargé d'Affaires. He had only recently arrived in Rome after a year's tour of duty in Berlin. Like myself, Kirk was "an old Roman hand," having been previously stationed in the Italian capital from 1928 until 1938, eight years of which we had spent working together, becoming close friends. William Phillips, although still Ambassador, was on an extended leave of absence at that time in the United States. In view of the deterioration of Italo-American relations, there was no longer much that a highly placed official such as an ambassador could do in Rome. Moreover, with local feeling running high against Americans, there was always the possibility that he might suffer some indignity despite the affection the Italians in general bore him personally. Therefore, the consensus among my colleagues in Rome was that it was more expedient that the Embassy be headed by a Chargé d'Affaires rather than an ambassador, so it looked as though Kirk might continue his role as Chief-of-Mission for some time.

In spite of growing anti-American sentiment, Italian friends who had known Kirk and myself before remained loyal to us. This was especially true of members of the Royal family. In the early days of 1941, I was invited several times to lunch or dine with Prince Philip of Hesse and his wife, the frail Princess Mafalda, the daughter of King Victor Emmanuel III and Queen Helena of Italy. She met a tragic end during the latter years of the war when, while a captive in a concentration camp in Germany, she was fatally injured during an Allied bombing raid. There were occasions also when the Queen of Italy herself would drop by Kirk's residence for a visit. Great secrecy was maintained in connection with these meetings, which could easily have been interpreted as something more than social, and of course no outsiders were invited to be present. The Queen was born the Princess of Montenegro; she believed that Great

Britain's lack of interest in her country was one of the main reasons why it had never regained its independence. Her well-known anti-British proclivities, however, obviously did not interfere with her contacts with the American diplomat.

Members of the Embassy also enjoyed social occasions with Alexander Kirk. In addition to pleasant dinners at his house, my wife and I had a standing invitation to attend the famous Rome Opera in Kirk's box at least three times a week. We never missed a performance, not so much because we were opera fans, but because there were few other diversions for Americans in Rome at that time. The curtain went up promptly at five o'clock in the afternoon in order to avoid the blackout. The elegant full evening dress which had been a must for those attending the opera in normal times was now clearly inappropriate. Kirk's hospitality compensated in part for our sorrow at being separated from Italian friends who were slowly becoming formal enemies.

Shortly after I joined the Embassy staff, we were surprised by Washington's announcement that Ambassador Phillips would after all be returning to Rome. The Ambassador was an intimate friend and long-standing confidant of President Roosevelt. As Ambassador to Italy, he had been remarkably successful in making contacts with both official and unofficial Rome. Furthermore, since the United States refused to recognize the new Italian "Empire" following Italy's conquest of Ethiopia in 1936, it would not be technically possible to appoint another American ambassador to the "King Emperor of Italy," as international protocol demanded. It was not difficult, therefore, to understand why the President decided to send Phillips back to Rome even with the risks such action might entail. In the face of the increasing tension between the United States and Italy, this move was regarded as one last effort on the President's part to maintain at least a semblance of high-level relations with Italy, in the desperate hope that there might be some useful outcome. The administration was making a major attempt to strengthen the Embassy's position at this critical hour by providing it with an ambassador who had always been sympathetic to the Italians, plus two subordinates, Kirk and myself, who had more experience in Italian affairs than anyone else in the United States Foreign Service. However, this rather special team was not destined to work together for long.

Immediately upon his arrival in Rome from the United States on January 15, 1941, Ambassador Phillips learned that the State Department was considering transferring Kirk from Rome to Cairo to be the U.S. envoy to Egypt and Saudi Arabia. Greatly disturbed by the prospect of losing Kirk's valuable experience, he sent a telegram to Washington strongly recommending that any thought of transferring Kirk be dropped. Instead, Phillips recommended that he be allowed to stay on in Rome as our representative to the Vatican City in the absence of Myron Taylor, who continued to remain in the United States. The Vatican and the British Government were also in favor of naming Kirk to the Vatican post and so informed the State Department. However, such approaches, and the desires of Ambassador Phillips were not sufficient to alter the decision of the Department of State. The Embassy was advised that no change could be made in the Department's plans, and that Kirk would be expected to proceed to Cairo as originally intended. The Department explained that Kirk would be far more valuable to the United States Government in Cairo than at the Vatican and suggested to Phillips that I fulfill the duties recommended for Kirk at the Holy See. On February 11, 1941, Kirk was officially transferred to Cairo.

During the first months of 1941, life along the Via Veneto and at the elegant Excelsior Hotel was still animated, although inevitably it had taken on some of the austerity of the times. The elderly Swiss Hall Porter, Herr Gubler, had just died. We had known him for years; he had been a landmark at the Excelsior Hotel since time immemorial. He was replaced behind the formidable concierge's desk by several eager young men of a different type. They were Italians and patriotic Fascists whose arrival removed from the lobby the atmosphere of warmth and friendliness created by the old man. They also caused my wife and myself, as well as other Americans, a certain amount of uneasiness, for we soon came to realize that these newcomers were closely observing our every move, no doubt reporting them to the Italian intelligence authorities.

The creature comforts at the Excelsior, a so-called "luxury" hotel in the capital of a country at war, were still very much in evidence. For instance, there was no lack of hot water at all times of the day or night. Food of every variety was plentiful, whereas I had seen that in hotels of equal category in neutral Switzerland, hot water was available to guests only three times a week and the meals were extremely simple, as food had been strictly rationed since the day war had been declared.

On the other hand, air raid alarms were not infrequent, and in order to be on the safe side, Rome would be alerted even when Allied raids were in progress as far away as Naples. The blackout in Rome was complete and served to minimize the usual social comings and goings for which the Via Veneto (even then the headquarters for the "Dolce Vita") and the Hotel Excelsior were famous. During the hours of darkness the circulation in the streets of the city was difficult since there were practically no taxi cabs and very few buses or streetcars. The air raid regulations in force at the Excelsior Hotel stipulated that whenever an alarm was heard at night, everyone was expected to get out of bed, dress and be ready to go down to the shelters, although actual descent was not required until the bursts of anti-aircraft fire began, which was not often. As a matter of fact, no one was really worried about Rome being bombed in those early days of the war, and most people felt that the strict black-out rules were a bit of an exaggeration.

During the first six months of 1941, Italo-American relations grew progressively worse. On March 11, Congress passed the Lend-Lease Act; this act excluded Italy from our lending programs, although she was not yet an official enemy of ours. On March 30, a law was passed to take over all Italian ships then on U.S. waters into protective custody. On April 2, Admiral Lais, the Italian Naval Attaché who was accused of ordering the crews of these vessels to commit sabotage, was expelled by our government from Washington. On May 27, President Roosevelt proclaimed "an unlimited national emergency," and on June 14, all Italian assets were frozen in the United States. By July 10, consular representations in both countries were completely closed, completing the gradual withdrawal which had begun on February 1.

The anti-American reaction in the Italian press to these various acts was instantaneous and violent, and the effect on the Italian people was considerable. As a result of this changing atmosphere, we found even our most intimate Italian friends becoming increasingly aloof and even hostile in their attitude toward us when we met one another in public. Obviously they were being conditioned by the official propagandists to regard Americans as enemies of Italy. Indeed, our friends felt that an outward display of hostility towards us was a necessary demonstration of their patriotism. In the dining room of the Excelsior, for example, they would sweep by our table, deliberately looking straight ahead without even glancing in our direction.

However, in their hearts most of them remained loyal to us,

and it was often possible to arrange private meetings between us
in apartments on the upper floors of the hotel. These meetings
were not without a certain risk, and there were a few uncomfortable moments. One evening after dinner, my wife and three
of her Italian friends, well-known figures in Italian society,
were playing bridge in the sitting room of our suite. Suddenly,
without a knock or warning of any kind, the door leading from
the outside corridor opened and a most handsome but official-
looking man, dressed in a dark suit, walked without hesitation
right up to the card table and stood there in silence, albeit
betraying a look of bewilderment. Jumping to the conclusion
that they were facing a member of the Italian Secret Police who
was coming to arrest them for associating with an American,
the Italian ladies rose from their chairs and prepared for the
worst. Their apprehension proved to be groundless, however, as
the intruder turned out to be none other than Prince Franz
Joseph II of Liechtenstein, who happened to be staying with his
family in the hotel. He had confused floors and had thought he
was coming into his own set of rooms, which were directly below
ours. His apologies were effusive. The ladies, happily relieved of
their fears, all agreed that the Prince could not have been more
charming, and thereupon resumed their bridge game.

There were others in the dining room besides ourselves who
suffered obvious slights from the Italians similar to ours. A
granddaughter of Queen Victoria, the English-born Queen Victoria Eugenia of Spain, known among her intimates as "Ena,"
was a truly remarkable personality, full of charm and humor,
who occupied the table next to ours in the dining room with
her lady-in-waiting, the Condessa Carmen Campo Alegre. The
Queen's ill-concealed leanings towards the Allied cause were
the talk of the town, so members of Roman society, passing her
table, refused to accord Her Majesty even a nod of recognition,

although she had two daughters who were married to Italian aristocrats and living in Italy. Eventually the Queen became *persona non grata* to the Italian government, and one year later was obliged to leave the country.

Phillips's telegram recommending that Kirk be named representative to the Vatican seemed to reawaken the interest of the Administration in the dormant Taylor mission. Three days after the Apostolic Delegate had made an approach to the State Department, the Under Secretary of State, Sumner Welles, wrote a letter to President Roosevelt suggesting that I be withdrawn from my post as Counselor of Embassy in Rome in order to resume the contacts with the Vatican which I had established the previous year when I had served as Taylor's assistant. About three weeks later, the President finally approved Welles's suggestion, and on February 20, 1941, the Department of State instructed me to leave my post as Counselor of Embassy in Rome and to resume my duties as Assistant to Mr. Taylor at the Vatican.

A few days previously, the appointment of George Wadsworth, then Consul General in Jerusalem, to be Counselor of Embassy in Rome had been announced in the press in the United States, which obviously meant that I was to be replaced. At the time, Ambassador Phillips had not been officially notified of my transfer to the Vatican, and he was unhappy thinking that the news about Wadsworth might mean that I was about to leave Rome altogether. He therefore sent a telegram to Washington urging that I not be moved:

> Sincerely hope the appointment of Wadsworth does not mean the transfer of Tittmann whose previous services in Rome give him exceptionally useful contacts at the Foreign Office and in Vatican circles. Former friendships

with Italians are indeed necessary in these difficult times
to carry on with any degree of utility the work of the
Embassy and a new Counselor would be at an enormous
disadvantage.

But it was already too late. Once again Washington was not
to be dissuaded from its prescribed course. For those of us in
Rome, it seemed strange that after what appeared to be an
attempt to fill the higher grades in the Rome embassy staff with
officers experienced in Italian affairs, Washington should so
abruptly have withdrawn two of them for service elsewhere.
Perhaps in view of Phillips's numerous contacts, to have added
Kirk's and mine would have been redundant. In any event, by
this time the authorities in Washington had concluded that
there was little to be done through the United States Embassy in
Rome to change the direction of Italy's path toward war with
the United States.

Although the Department's instruction assumed that I
would immediately transfer from the Embassy to the Vatican
mission, this step was postponed for two months since Phillips
had requested that I continue my duties as Counselor until the
arrival of Wadsworth, who had been delayed. As the Department did not mention any new credentials for me at the Holy
See, when the time came for the transfer on April 21, 1941, I
simply wrote a note to the Cardinal Secretary of State informing
him that as of that day I had resumed my duties as Myron Taylor's assistant. And, at the bottom of the letter, beneath my signature, my new title was added, "Foreign Service Officer on
Special Duty."

Because of the delicacy with which the Administration in
Washington was still obliged to handle all matters concerning
the United States representation at the Holy See, and in order

to keep everything on a strictly nonofficial and informal basis, I was told to set up an office in Rome entirely separate from the Embassy. In my correspondence with the Vatican and with the general public, my letterhead would carry only the words "Foreign Service of the United States," the address of my office and my new title appearing below my signature at the end of my letters. However, regular Embassy stationery could be used for communications to the Department of State. My salary and allowances continued to be paid from normal sources. But again, with the purpose of making my duties appear as unofficial as possible, the rent of the separate office and other extraordinary expenses, including an annual representation allowance of $460.00, were to be charged to the President's discretionary fund, and not to the regular State Department budget.

After my wife left in April to join the children in Switzerland, I established my office in a room adjoining the suite we had occupied in the Hotel Excelsior. The Embassy Chancery provided me with office furniture and assigned me a full-time stenographer, Nicolina Flammia, from its staff. We kept regular office hours, from nine in the morning to one, and from four in the afternoon until seven in the evening.

In the early days of my official relations with Vatican officials, I found them uncertain with regard to United States war policy. They had been impressed by Axis propaganda insisting that a democracy such as ours could not adjust itself to the realities of a world war; that, as a people, we were disunited and that we cared more for peace at any price than for the preservation by force of ideals and freedom; in sum, that isolationism was the prevailing sentiment in the United States of America. The Vatican had also received warnings that influential members of the Catholic hierarchy in the United States were opposed to our entering the war. The effect of the German propaganda on political leaders in continental Europe, including Italy and the Holy See, understandably worried President Roosevelt and the Administration in general. This nervousness was apparent in the President's address of March 15 before the White House Correspondents' Association warning against this German propaganda. On April 26, I received the following telegram from the Secretary of State, Cordell Hull, expressing continuing concern that our position be made clear:

> At this crucial period in the struggle against totalitarian world aggression, I wish to emphasize the obligation resting upon every representative of this government abroad to contribute in every way within his power to the success of that struggle. The government and people of the United States have made it abundantly clear that we do not intend to stand in the sidelines, but that on the contrary we do intend to play our part in resisting the forces of aggression. It is therefore incumbent upon every representative of this government abroad and, in fact, upon every American citizen abroad, to reflect in his own bearing and in his conversation with whomever he may come in contact, the absolute determination of his government and his country to see this thing through to a successful conclusion. You need have no hesitancy in expressing our determination and our convictions in the strongest terms.

I was now confronted with the problem of persuading the Holy See that the United States would never agree to a Nazi victory of any kind.

At the end of April, I met by chance in the corridors of the Secretariat of State Archbishop Filippo Bernardini, at the time the Apostolic Nuncio in Bern, Switzerland, but who had been for several years previously attached to the Apostolic Delegation in Washington. He claimed, therefore, to know the popular feeling in the United States well. He was frankly pessimistic regarding the possibilities of a British victory in Europe even with our aid and he therefore hoped for an early compromise peace as the best solution. When I impressed upon him, as I had upon other Vatican dignitaries, our determination to defeat the aggressors, he replied that he fully realized that this was what we intended to do, but that he was skeptical of our ability to carry out our plans, chiefly because of opposition at home which he, as a former resident of the United States, could feel was considerable. I then asked him how, as a Roman Catholic churchman, he could possibly be in favor of a compromise which would mean a Hitler-controlled Europe and the continued harassment of Catholics, to which he made the amazing reply that, taking the long view, he welcomed a certain amount of persecution of the Church for its own good and that he was certain that within a few years the Nazi prejudice against Catholics was destined to die out. He added that in his opinion the elimination of Nazi personalities, which seemed to be one of the aims of the Allies, was not a prerequisite to arranging a compromise peace, because these personalities represented only the shell of the Nazi substance, which at present was disappearing in Germany, just as the substance of Fascism was now hardly visible any longer in Italy.

I saw the Cardinal Secretary of State, Maglione, who was responsible for the Vatican's foreign relations, for the first time on April 26. He asked me whether I could sum up for him in a few words the current war policy of the United States. So many diplomats, he said, had asked him questions on the subject, and he was frankly at a loss for adequate replies. My answer was that it was my conviction that we would never allow Hitler to win the war, no matter how long it might last. To this statement of mine he made no comment. The demeanor of Cardinal Maglione appeared to me graver than on any of the occasions I had met with him the year before, and it was obvious that he was discouraged. He said that no word regarding the prospects for peace had come to him so far from any direction and that he had heard nothing of any project looking to a compromise between the belligerents in the near future.

Another striking religious personality, although not a member of the Vatican family, also expressed his doubts and uncertainties when I went to see him on May 2. This was the Most Reverend Vladimir Ledochowski, Superior General of the Jesuit Order with headquarters in Rome. He was Polish by birth, imbued with the fighting spirit of the Jesuits, in contrast to the more cautious attitude of the Holy See. Father Ledochowski's influence throughout the Catholic world was so powerful that he was often referred to as the "Black Pope" (his soutane was black, whereas the Pope's was white). I expressed to him in the strongest possible terms our determination to win the war, but while he willingly applauded our position, he indicated to me that he was much afraid of the "Fifth Column," the pro-Axis groups everywhere, even inside the Vatican itself, and especially within the United States and Latin America. He suspected that Cardinal William O'Connell of Boston and Archbishop John Timothy McNicholas of Cincinnati, who was born in Ireland, were not sufficiently convinced that Hitler was out to destroy the Catholic Church. Both of these prelates were of Irish blood and for this reason were not enthusiastic about supporting the British, who were Ireland's traditional enemies. As for Latin America, Father Ledochowski expressed concern about reports from southern Brazil and from the Argentine Republic where the Foreign Minister, Enrique Ruis Guinazu, was "a good Catholic and an honest man," but "impressionable and needed to be watched." The Superior General believed, however, that everything would be all right in Latin America if the United States exercised unflagging vigilance to prevent "Fifth Column" corruption. Ledochowski was fully aware of the risks he himself had taken in opposing the Nazis, but was ready, he said, for martyrdom if necessary.

The Pope first received me alone on May 5 in his library two weeks after I had taken over my new job at the Vatican. Pursuant to my instructions, I told the Holy Father that we were determined to play an active role in opposing the forces of aggression and that the United States and the American people were determined to see the struggle through to a successful conclusion, emphasizing the great power of the United States and the extent of our efforts. The Pope asked whether this meant that we were prepared to enter the war if necessary. I replied that we would not shrink from such an issue should it arise, but that it was my own personal opinion that to all intents and purposes we were already in the war. His Holiness then said, "Having visited the United States myself, I am convinced of the power of your country, but in the event that your assistance were to arrive too late to prevent the defeat of England in Europe, what would then be the position of the United States?" To this I answered that the phrase "too little and too late" did not figure in our calculations, but if by some stretch of the imagination that should prove to be the case, we would nevertheless continue to carry on the struggle by ourselves no matter how long it might take until victory over the aggressors had been achieved. The Pope's comment on this last statement was "very important, very important indeed."

I added that a compromise with the Nazis for us was unthinkable, since there was not a man, woman or child in the

United States who had confidence in Hitler's word. The Holy Father replied that his dealings with Hitler had also led him to the conclusion that the Fuehrer's word could not be relied upon. The Concordat between Germany and the Holy See, which he said had been asked for originally by the Germans themselves, was being repeatedly violated since Hitler's rise to power. He then asked about reports of popular opposition in the United States to our standing up against the Germans, especially the influence of Charles Lindbergh, with whom he had talked when they were in Berlin together. I assured His Holiness that these reports were only rumors and could be safely discounted, although the Italian press was playing them up for all they were worth in order to impress the public in Italy. Throughout this part of the conversation the Pope displayed intense interest, but maintained a completely neutral attitude, and his observations were limited to "very interesting" or "very important." There was no word, not even a flicker of the eye, that might have been inter-preted as approval of our position as I had outlined it to him.

We then discussed relations between Germany and the Holy See, which the Pope frankly admitted were entirely unsatisfac-tory. He had done everything in his power to bring about an improvement, but all his efforts so far had failed and things were going from bad to worse. The Holy Father felt, however, that as Head of the Church, it was still his duty not to refuse to receive Catholic members of the German armed forces visiting Rome and he would continue to do so. With regard to relations between the Holy See and Italy, the Italians were allowing him "freedom of action" and, as evidence of this, he pointed to the fact that his Easter Message had been broadcast by all Italian radio stations. He acknowledged that incidents such as Fascist objections to Vatican Radio broadcasts or to articles in the Vati-can newspaper, *l'Osservatore Romano,* which were considered to be anti-Axis were bound to arise from time to time, but were of minor importance. In spite of these assurances, I had the impression that the Pope was somewhat uneasy as to his future relations with Italy as well.

Two days later I went to see Monsignor Giovanni Battista Montini, Substitute Secretary of State of His Holiness. He reported that the Pope was very pleased with the audience I had just had with him and that I had left a good impression. I gave Monsignor Montini my usual rundown on the strong stand we were taking in the United States against the aggressor nations, but added that it was surprising to me that my statements seemed to have had so little visible effect on any of the Vatican dignitaries with whom I had spoken, especially since it should be clear to everybody by this time that the only hope for the Church lay in a final Anglo-American victory no matter what it might suffer in the meantime. But here again, consistent with the impression I had gained during my meetings with the Pope and the Cardinal Secretary of State, no reaction, favorable or otherwise, could be detected. When I referred to the likelihood of our participation in the conflict, Montini's only comment was, "Although the Church recognizes the possibility of a just war, it must always disapprove of the killing of human beings."

While the Vatican, in order to maintain its neutral status, could not afford to take a forthright position in favor of any one country, I had come to the conclusion that the true reason for its noncommittal attitude stemmed not from this, but rather from the conviction that as things were going then, a German victory in Europe was inevitable and that the Pope, responsible for the welfare of the Church, was obliged to shape his policies accordingly as best he could, always in the interests of the millions of Roman Catholics. The recent German invasions of the Balkans, the Fascist claims that the people of the United States, including important members of the Catholic clergy, were not wholly behind President Roosevelt's hard line against the Nazis, and the feeling that in any event American aid to Great Britain was destined to arrive too late, had done much to strengthen this conviction. In this the Holy See was only reflecting opinion that currently prevailed in high Italian circles. The Vatican apparently felt that the quicker a peaceful settlement was reached, the more likely something could be salvaged for the Church. Hence I detected a certain sense of disappointment in those with whom I talked that the United States seemed to have chosen to play the part of a belligerent rather than a peacemaker. However, I believed that, in spite of the sensation of defeatism and fear forced upon the Holy See by events, my Vatican friends, deep down in their hearts, did realize that the only hope for the Church to avoid the neo-paganism of the Germans and the atheistic communism of the Russians was an Anglo-Saxon victory.

To sum up, I reported to Washington that in my opinion 1) the last thing the Vatican would welcome would be a Hitler victory, 2) in spite of my efforts so far to convince the Holy See that the Allies were bound to win in the end, the worst—an Axis success—was still feared and 3) at the moment the Vatican would actively support any compromise proposal to end the war that had even the faintest hope of success.

In order to convince the Holy See that we had the material means to defeat the aggressors, I requested the Department of State to furnish me a detailed list of our war preparations which I might show to the Holy See. The State Department's reply supported the line I had taken in my conversations at the Vatican and provided me with a prodigious list of figures describing the rearmament activities of the United States. I gave these statistics, as well as a useful study on the same subject prepared by the American Embassy in Rome, to the Pope and other high-ranking Vatican authorities. I also arranged to provide the diplomatic representations to the Holy See of the principal European and Latin American countries with the same information. When I saw him again, Monsignor Montini displayed for the first time a certain amount of enthusiasm for our war efforts and indicated that he was particularly struck by the magnitude of the defense appropriations which appeared to be astronomical, as I had been careful to convert the huge dollar numbers into Italian lire at the black market rate. In a memorandum dated May 8 to Ray Atherton, Chief of the Division of European Affairs, Under Secretary of State Welles wrote:

It is, in my opinion, much more useful sending Tittmann weekly summaries of the progress we are making here in rearmament and any salient features that develop from day to day indicating the strong policy which this Government is adopting, than to supply information of that character to our Embassy in Rome which cannot find any outlet for it under present conditions.

After President Roosevelt made his dramatic radio address from the White House on May 27, 1941, proclaiming the existence of "Unlimited National Emergency" for the country, I delivered copies of the text of the speech to the Vatican Secretariat of State. Cardinal Maglione, to whom I had personally handed a copy, told me that he had already read the Italian translation which was broadcast from the United States and transcribed for him by Vatican Radio technicians. His only comment on the speech was the usual "very interesting." Monsignor Montini, when he received me, seemed more at liberty to express himself. He said that both the Pope and the Cardinal Secretary of State had found the speech "most interesting" and "very strong," and that in general it had made a deep impression in Vatican circles.

Based on "The Unlimited National Emergency" which he had declared on May 27, 1941, President Roosevelt issued an Executive Order the following month on June 14 "freezing" the assets in the United States of various European countries, including Italy. At first the Vatican wondered whether the action against Italy might not comprise its own funds as well, but the Apostolic Delegate in Washington soon notified the Vatican that the United States Government had informed him that the assets of the State of the Vatican City would not be "frozen" under the provisions relating to Italy, but that a list thereof should be submitted by the Vatican to the Treasury Department so that the appropriate licenses could be issued.

Nevertheless there were further complications. Engineer Enrico Pietro Galeazzi, the administrative head of the Vatican City and a close confidant of the Pope, called me to his office in the Governor's Palace in the Vatican City on the afternoon of June 19, 1941. He told me that the Holy Father wished to see me immediately on a strictly confidential matter. He offered to conduct me forthwith to the Pope's private apartment on the top floor of the Vatican Palace, which was used exclusively for meeting with his immediate family or with his intimate friends. We were directed to the elevator reserved for the Pope's use alone, which was well hidden in a far corner of the building. On leaving the elevator we were ushered into a living room which surprised me by resembling those of the average Rome apartment. There were simple dark heavy oak furnishings, in distinct contrast to the glittering reception rooms of the Pope's official quarters on the floor below. I sat down at one end of a large sofa not far from the door, and waited for the Holy Father to make his appearance. When he entered the living room, clad in his usual white soutane and white silk skullcap, I naturally rose to greet him. But he motioned me to remain where I was while he took his place at the opposite end of the sofa.

He began the interview by saying that he had been very much relieved to learn of the decision of the United States Government to exclude the assets of the Holy See from any "freezing" action. However, one matter was still of concern to him and this was the reason why he had asked me to come to see him. He explained that he was worried about certain special accounts in New York banks. Some were administered by Archbishop Spellman, but there was also another personal and secret account of his own about which Spellman knew nothing. The Pope asserted that all the funds mentioned were being used exclusively for charitable purposes. The Holy Father requested that I immediately wire Mr. Taylor in New York, asking him to get in touch with Archbishop Spellman to ensure that these private accounts, like the official ones of the Holy See, be listed with the Treasury Department, thus ensuring their freedom of movement. I promised the Holy Father that I would do everything he asked.

We also discussed briefly U.S. rearmament. Although the Pope was careful not to express an opinion which might be interpreted as favoring one side or the other in the conflict, I found him most eager for additional news and statistics of our preparations to defeat the aggressors, and he seemed to have grasped in a surprising manner the significance of the memorandum detailing our war efforts. The Holy Father appeared to be still greatly impressed by the military might of Germany and spoke especially of the enormous booty that had fallen into German hands during the past year. He again complained bitterly of the treatment the Church had been receiving in Germany and stated that, although the situation continued to deteriorate, he saw nothing he could do at present to reverse this trend. He added that relations between the Holy See and Italy were not exactly satisfactory, but could not, of course, be compared with the desperate situation in Germany.

As we parted, the Holy Father warned me that the information he had just given me should be held in the strictest confidence, since general knowledge of the existence and use of the New York accounts could be misinterpreted, especially by the Nazis. He also made it clear that he thought it wise not to mention the fact that we had seen each other secretly in his private quarters, as this could be misconstrued as well.

As far as I know, the requests of the Holy Father were complied with in Washington and New York. As it turned out, this was the only time I was to have such an informal interview with His Holiness during my six years with the Taylor mission to the Vatican.

Rumors continued to circulate in Rome that certain members of the Catholic hierarchy were not wholeheartedly supporting the United States Government policy to defeat the Nazis. Two American prelates, Cardinal O'Connell of Boston and Archbishop McNicholas of Cincinnati, had already been mentioned to me by the Father General of the Jesuits as belonging to this category, while the Vatican believed that Archbishop Michael Joseph Curley of Baltimore, Maryland, and Archbishop Francis I. Beckman of Dubuque, Iowa, could also be included. I had therefore suggested to the Department of State in late May that I be authorized to consult with the Pope on the subject of converting the "doubting Thomases" among the American Catholic clergy. The Department advised me a few days later that the matter had been referred to Myron Taylor, who was in Washington at the time.

Taylor called on the Apostolic Delegate to convey President Roosevelt's fears that some members of the Catholic hierarchy in the United States were not sufficiently aware of the spiritual dangers resulting from the spread of Nazism and also to express the President's disapproval of those priests who had actually declared themselves in favor of Germany. The President was upset by reports that there was opposition to the policies and actions of the United States Government among the bishops. Mr. Taylor noted that the pro-isolationist "America First Committee" had distributed on May 23 thousands of copies of a passage, taken out of context, from the Statement published on April 23 by the Board of the National Catholic Welfare Conference, which gave the impression to the public that the members of the Board were seeking peace, were advocating isolationism and were opposed to the Government's foreign policy. Mr. Taylor mentioned as an aside that a large number of the American hierarchy were either Irish-born or of Irish descent, which made it easier for them to refuse to support any American help for the British, their traditional enemy.

Monsignor Cicognani, reporting to the Vatican regarding Mr. Taylor's remarks, denied that the pronouncements of April 23 by the bishops, both individually and collectively, could be construed in any way as being in favor of the Nazis. Their attitude, he explained, was well expressed when they declared themselves unqualified to suggest directives on political or military matters. Cicognani mentioned that the hierarchy had been criticized, sometimes malevolently, by various groups, especially committees of women and mothers, for not coming out openly against the intervention of the United States in the war, but the bishops invariably refused to declare themselves either *pro* or *contra*, since the questions raised were none of their business and also because they wished to avoid any appearance of opposition to the Government.

Cicognani did admit, however, to Mr. Taylor that there were a few prelates (including Cardinal O'Connell of Boston and

Archbishop Curley of Baltimore) who had spoken in public against the United States entering the war, but none of these had said anything in favor of Germany and it was well known that they harbored the same feelings towards "dictators" as did the rest of the population of the United States. Archbishop Cicognani then observed that because the members of the hierarchy were so numerous (116 bishops and archbishops in residence, and more than 34,000 priests), it was inevitable that there should be some divergence of opinion among them, but that as regards international politics they had all proved themselves to be fine examples of discipline. Under the circumstances, the Department of State advised me that probably no useful purpose could be served by my approaching the Holy Father personally on the matter. The rumors I had mentioned in my telegram now appeared to have been exaggerated. Since I had been instrumental in briefing Vatican officials on the extent of our war preparations and helpful in clarifying the views held by the Holy See with regard to the alleged isolationist sentiments of the people and the Catholic clergy in the United States, I began to realize that my presence at the Vatican at this troubled moment was proving to be of some use to my country.

As it began to appear that relations between Italy and the United States might be severed, Monsignor Montini told me on April 30, 1941, that the Vatican would agree to a transfer of my office and residence from the Excelsior Hotel in Rome into the Vatican City. He warned that communication from the Vatican City to the outside world would be difficult and that I would not be permitted to file telegrams in code. I would also, he said, be obliged to enter into a "gentlemen's agreement" not to send out information of a military character. Communications would be effected by Vatican pouch twice weekly, but should Switzerland become isolated, diplomats inside the Vatican could lose touch with their governments. I informed Washington of Montini's remarks.

The State Department authorized me on June 2 to inform the Vatican that the United States was grateful for the Vatican offer of hospitality, particularly in view of my "unusual status," and that I should accept the offer should the occasion arise. Montini remarked that this demonstrated the importance attached by my government to maintaining direct relations with the Holy See at this time.

Again on July 8, the Vatican reassured me of its willingness to receive me inside its walls, but two weeks later Cardinal Maglione, perhaps having second thoughts on my "unusual status," called me to his office and suggested that I should reside in Switzerland and keep in touch with the Holy See through the Papal representative there, just as the diplomats of the two Central Powers, Prussia and Bavaria, had done during the First World War. Maglione had been the Apostolic Nuncio in Bern during the 1920s and was therefore able to assure me that this arrangement would work out well. I gathered that Maglione was pushing for the Bern alternative, hoping that in adopting this solution the embarrassment of adding yet another Allied official to the "nest of spies" already in the Vatican City could be averted, putting less strain on its delicate relations with the Axis powers. The State Department nevertheless preferred that I move into the Vatican. However, an incident concerning the Yugoslav representation to the Holy See raised doubts in my mind about my own chances of entering the Vatican City as a permanent resident at some future date.

The Germans had invaded Yugoslavia from Hungary, Bulgaria, and Rumania on April 6, 1941. After the invasion, King Peter and his government fled to Athens and then to Jerusalem for a stay of two months before proceeding to London to join other governments-in-exile. On April 10, only four days after the German attack, the "Independent State of Croatia," for the most part Roman Catholic, was carved out of former Yugoslav territory on an understanding between Hitler and Mussolini that it would eventually become a vassal state of Italy. Its independence was formally proclaimed in Zagreb, the capital of Croatia, on April 14 by Colonel Slavko Kvarternik in the name of the President and Prime Minister, Dr. Ante Pavelic, a professed Roman Catholic, and immediately recognized by the two Axis dictators.

Count Niko Mirosevic Sorgo, Yugoslav Minister to the Holy See, continued to represent his country as it was before the German invasion, in accordance with the Vatican's policy not to recognize a newly formed state until after a peace treaty had been signed. Although a Croat by birth of aristocratic Dalmatian lineage, Mirosevic could not bear to see Yugoslavia divided and was bitterly opposed to the Pavelic regime. He informed the Vatican frequently that the Royal Yugoslav government-in-exile under King Peter II protested the creation of Croatia as an independent kingdom and requested that the protest be made known to the Italian Government by the Holy See. Mirosevic also disagreed with any Vatican intention to send a Papal representative to Zagreb no matter what his title might be, as such action could publicly signify the quasi-recognition by the Holy See of the new political situation.

It was now Pavelic's turn to complain to the Holy See, criticizing its lack of interest in the new state. The Italian Ambassador to the Vatican, Dr. Bernardo Attolico, informed Monsignor Tardini on July 13 that he had heard that Pavelic was furious because an Apostolic Nunciature had been established in Slovakia together with a Slovak Legation at the Vatican immediately after that country had declared itself independent, whereas the

Vatican had refused diplomatic relations with Croatia, although, like Slovakia, it was also a Catholic country that had just received its independence. The Holy See then agreed to send an unofficial representative to Zagreb to be accredited to the Croatian hierarchy, and to receive an unofficial representative from Croatia, only to discuss Church affairs.

The individual chosen to represent the Holy See in the Croat capital was the Abbot of the Monastery of Montevergine, Father Giuseppe Marcone of the Order of Saint Benedict. The first private Croatian representative at the Vatican was Dr. Nikola Rusinovic, who was American born and, because of the Vatican's attitude of nonrecognition, found it difficult even to contact members of the Secretariat of State. He was replaced on October 1, 1942, by Prince Erwin Charles Lobkowicz, who already enjoyed an "in" at the Vatican, since for several years he had been one of the Pope's many "Privy Chamberlains of Sword and Cape Participating." This gave Lobkowicz a better chance than his predecessor to be received by the Holy Father. Lobkowicz, who came from a well-known Austro-German aristocratic family, had been an officer in the Austro-Hungarian army in World War One, after which he settled in Croatia. The Croat Lobkowicz and his Hungarian colleague at the Holy See, Baron Gabriel Apor, who had been a friend of mine before the war broke out, were working together to convince the Holy See that their two Catholic countries constituted a bulwark of Christianity against Bolshevism. They expressed the hope that, in return, the Holy See would give special attention to their interests when the time came for peace negotiations. But the names of Rusinovic, Lobkowicz and Father Marcone never appeared in the official Vatican list of diplomats.

Italy had not yet declared war on Yugoslavia, but the Italian Government nevertheless announced that it approved of what the Germans were doing in that country both politically and militarily, saying "Italy has decided to act with her military, naval and air forces in strict collaboration with those of Germany." Both Germany and Italy henceforth regarded the state of Yugoslavia as nonexistent.

Under the circumstances, Mirosevic felt uncomfortable residing on Italian soil and was able to arrange with the Holy See for himself and his family to move into the Vatican City just as soon as accommodations could be available. Mirosevic also arranged for his Legation Secretary, Kosta M. Zukic, and his wife to move into the Vatican. After extensive alterations paid for by the Vatican, a large apartment of twelve rooms on the second floor of the "palazzino" or annex of Santa Marta across the courtyard from the main building was readied for the minister and his family, while a very small one with only two rooms on the ground floor was prepared for the Zukics. The furniture and other household effects of the Mirosevics and the Zukics were transported from Rome to the Vatican City and they were all prepared to move into their new lodgings on May 5 when they were informed by Cardinal Canali, the chief of the governing body of the Vatican City, that they would not be expected to make the move since the Italian authorities had decided to permit them to remain unmolested in their residences outside. The Holy See, having evidently changed its mind, had requested that the Italian Government allow Mirosevic and members of the staff of the Yugoslav Legation to remain in Rome in accordance with the provisions of the Lateran Treaty, since a state of war did not formally exist between Italy and Yugoslavia. On May 1, the Vatican was informed by the Italian Embassy that permission had been granted on orders from Mussolini himself, who was anxious to avoid any violation of the Lateran Treaty.

Mirosevic made it clear that he intended to accept the Holy See's hospitality even though the Italian Government had become more lenient, but he was advised by the Cardinal Secretary of State, as well as by the British Minister, D'Arcy Osborne, representing his diplomatic colleagues, to avail himself of the Italian Government's permission to remain in Rome. Maglione and Osborne were both anxious to see the terms in the Lateran Treaty regarding the protection of diplomats complied with by the Italian authorities. Mirosevic finally decided to follow their advice. Things went well enough for the diplomats of the Yugoslav Legation residing in Rome until July 2, when the Holy See was surprised to learn that the Italian Government, at the insistence of the Italian military authorities, had reversed its former position and that Mirosevic and his staff would now be obliged to move into the Vatican City, and with the least possible delay. The Holy See, however, hesitated to take the action demanded, since it would mean a violation of the Lateran Treaty not only harmful to the interests of the Vatican, but to those of Italy as well. On July 16, the Italians repeated their demand, but the Vatican preferred to continue the discussions with the hope that an agreement might be reached.

But then the bomb fell. On July 24, the Italian Embassy, under special orders from Mussolini, requested Cardinal Maglione to instruct Minister Mirosevic to leave Italy immediately. The Cardinal refused, stating that he could not do so without first knowing the reasons for the Italian attitude, but that the Minister in any event would be accepted in the Vatican City, should he ask for asylum there. The Pope approved what Maglione said. The next day, Maglione was informed that the Italian security services, accusing the Minister of espionage, required his expulsion from Italy and refused to allow him to take refuge inside the Vatican City. The Italian Embassy also told Maglione that its government planned to remain faithful to the provisions of the Lateran Treaty in spite of the present incident, which had only to do with the security of the country. The Cardinal replied with a mildly worded protest.

On July 25, the Yugoslav Legation was picketed by Italian soldiers and entered by members of the secret police. Mirosevic himself was held incommunicado, his passport taken from him, and he was told that he would have to leave Italian territory at once, but that he could not take refuge inside the Vatican City since Yugoslavia had ceased to exist and he had therefore lost his status as a diplomat representing an independent state. My British colleague, as well as other Allied diplomats, went immediately to the Vatican Secretariat of State to protest this blatant violation of diplomatic rights under the Lateran Accords. Although the United States had not yet entered the war and I was still living in the Excelsior Hotel in Rome, I nevertheless hurried over to the Vatican in order to join in the protest, as I was interested in preventing the acceptance by the Holy See of any Italian Government policy that might hinder my taking up residence inside the Vatican City at some future date.

Cardinal Maglione told us that, according to the Italian Embassy to the Holy See, the Yugoslav Minister, who openly visited his Allied colleagues in the Vatican City, was suspected of espionage against Italy and that for reasons of national security he would be obliged to leave the country. The Italian Embassy had requested the Holy See at first to cooperate by demanding that the Minister leave. Maglione had immediately replied that the accusation against Mirosevic was unbelievable, since the honor and correct behavior of the distinguished diplomat in question was well known to everyone, and that in any case documentary proof in support of the grave accusation was needed. He added that while the Vatican could not possibly ask the Minister to leave Italy, it was ready to receive him and his family inside the Vatican City without the consent of the Italian Government. Later, the Italian Government confirmed the accusation of espionage to the Vatican, but declared that for security reasons the Italian authorities concerned were not in a position to make known the confidential proofs in their posses-sion. However, I myself learned from private Vatican sources that the Italians had in mind the alleged activities of Mirosevic in a secret intelligence center in Rome which was sending infor-mation out of the country.

In the end, at the instigation of the Italian Government only, with the Vatican standing aside, the Minister was forced to quit Italian territory and to proceed to a country other than the State of the Vatican City. On July 30, Mirosevic left Rome for Bern, Switzerland, and later settled in Lisbon.

The Holy See, embarrassed by the incident and wishing to demonstrate its esteem for Minister Mirosevic, addressed an offi-cial note to him on July 26 expressing its profound regret, not only for the enforced removal from Rome of a duly accredited diplo-mat, but also for not being able to receive him inside the Vatican City. Zukic, the Legation Secretary, decided to take no chances and on August 18, 1941, moved into the Vatican City with his wife. The Zukics occupied the same small apartment which had originally been set aside for them two months before. They brought with them the archives of the Legation. For the remain-der of the current conflict, Mirosevic continued to be recognized by the Holy See as the legitimate Yugoslav Minister and kept in constant touch with the Secretariat of State and his own legation at the Vatican through the Apostolic Nunciature in Lisbon and directly with the Yugoslav Government-in-exile in London.

The Mirosevic matter gave me much cause for uneasiness. It seemed to me that the Italian Government could question my "unusual" status of not being a fully accredited diplomat, to keep me from joining my colleagues already residing within the Vatican walls in Santa Marta.

Mirosevic's misfortunes turned out to be my father's blessing, as the Vatican informed him that the apartment prepared for the Yugoslavs, the most spacious of the diplomatic residences inside the Holy City, would be kept available for him in the event of a break in relations between the United States and Italy.

When the school year ended in June, my father's assignment to the Vatican mission had clearly become a long-term matter, and would probably involve his moving into the Vatican City should the United States and Italy go to war. Maintaining a home in Geneva no longer made sense, particularly as my mother felt it her duty to be at the side of her diplomat husband. Thus the Geneva interlude came to an end in September, when we moved out of Campagne Mallet and the family furniture was shipped to the United States.

My mother joined my father at the Excelsior in Rome, after enrolling her sons at Le Rosey boarding school. I recall being pleased with this decision, as I had pleasant memories of my previous stay. It was probably more difficult for my younger brother Barclay, who was only nine years old, but he soon adjusted to his new surroundings. Because of the war, the number of students at Le Rosey remained well below normal, so that a certain familylike atmosphere prevailed. The younger boys received special attention from Madame Carnal, the wife of the owner and director of the school. A charming American lady, she would drop by the bedrooms of the "juniors" shortly before the lights out deadline, to chat with the younger boys and make sure that they were not homesick. For them, she became a much-loved second mother.

In June 1941, the German Army invaded the Soviet Union and rapidly scored some notable victories. The Myron Taylor mission's principal task during the closing months of 1941 was to obtain as much support as possible from the Vatican for President Roosevelt's policy of assisting Germany's new enemy.

After the Nazi attack on Russia, President Roosevelt realized that without large-scale military and other aid from the United

States, the chances of a Soviet victory over the Nazis would be slim indeed. The difficulties encountered in financing this aid seemed at first insurmountable, so that Roosevelt became convinced that the inclusion of Russia in the Lend-Lease program already applied to other countries would be the only solution. However, he was aware that unless authorization from Congress could be obtained, the necessary aid would not be forthcoming. Congress was in no frame of mind to agree, influenced as it was by strong anti-Soviet convictions among large groups of American citizens, who, mostly for religious motives, simply did not approve of helping Communists in any way. This was especially true in the case of American Roman Catholics, who had been much impressed by the anti-Communist Encyclical *Divini Redemptoris* (Of the Divine Redeemer) of Pope Pius XI, published on March 19, 1937, containing a broad condemnation of atheistic communism and forbidding all Catholics to collaborate with it. The passage referred to in the encyclical stated, "See to it, Venerable Brethren, that the Faithful do not allow themselves to be deceived! Communism is intrinsically wrong, and no one who would save Christian Civilization may collaborate with it in any undertaking whatsoever."

At the beginning of the Second World War, Communist militant atheism was still regarded in the Vatican as more obnoxious than modern paganism in Germany. There was always the chance that the Nazis, confronted by the power of the Catholic Church in Germany, might change their policy of persecution, while in Russia, where the cult had disappeared altogether, there was little or no hope for improvement.

President Roosevelt, confronted with the Lend-Lease for Russia problem, decided to do everything possible to minimize the anti-Soviet sentiment in the United States. First, he wanted to suggest to the Pope that the Vatican take measures to moderate the outlook of American Catholics and second, he hoped to endeavor through diplomatic channels to persuade the Soviet government to speak out openly in favor of religious toleration in Russia. Since the matter was pressing, the President requested Myron Taylor to return to Rome early in September 1941 in order to resume contacts with the Holy Father, especially on the subject of Catholic opinion in the United States. Mr. Taylor, accompanied by his wife Annabel, arrived in Rome on September 9 and remained for two weeks. Ambassador Taylor was received by the Pope three times during his stay.

I myself had already raised the burning question of the future of religion in Russia in a telegram that I had sent to Washington on July 24. I asked whether it would not be possible for our government to declare that in lending our support to Russia and in preparation for the peace, it hoped that the Soviet Government would abandon its attitude of religious and political intolerance and adopt instead policies that were more liberal and humane. I said that some such pronouncement would have a reassuring effect on the Holy See, on Catholic countries everywhere and on all decent people as well. I added that it would be helpful if the Department would let me have any evidence that might come to hand of increased religious tolerance in Russia. The Department's reply of July 31 was anything but hopeful. I was informed that no such indications of religious tolerance had been received. The State Department went on to say that, while it sympathized with the spirit that prompted my suggestion, it did not believe that it would serve a constructive purpose or be advisable at that time to make any statement appearing to pressure the Soviet government to change certain internal policies.

It came as a complete surprise to me when I learned that Taylor, at his first audience, had delivered a letter to the Pope dated September 3, labeled "personal" and signed by Roosevelt, sounding a definite note of optimism as to the future of religion in the Soviet Union. In his communcation, which had been drafted entirely by himself, the President said: "Insofar as I am informed, churches in Russia are open," stating further his belief that there was "a real possibility that Russia may, as a result of the present conflict, recognize freedom of religion." The President added that the only weapon the Russian dictatorship used outside its borders was its Communist propaganda to break down certain forms of government, religious beliefs, etc. in other countries. On the other hand, he pointed out that the Nazis, while utilizing the same type of propaganda, were also engaging in military aggression for the purpose of world conquest. "I believe that the survival of Russia," the President concluded, "is less dangerous to religion to the Church as such, to humanity in general, than would be the survival of the German form of dictatorship. Furthermore, it is my belief that leaders of all churches in the United States should recognize these facts clearly and should not close their eyes to these basic matters and by their present attitudes (anti-Soviet) on this question directly assist Germany on her present objectives."

The contents of the President's letter were hardly in agreement with the information on Russia that had been assembled at the Vatican—quite the contrary.

Monsignor Domenico Tardini prepared at least seven memoranda for the archives containing the Pope's reflections as well as his own regarding various aspects of Mr. Taylor's discussion at the Vatican, especially President Roosevelt's views on Communist Russia at the time. They were amazingly frank and sometimes even humorous. Nobody could have been better qualified for this task than Tardini. He not only held the number-two position, Secretary for Extraordinary Affairs, in the Secretariat of State after the Secretary himself, Cardinal Maglione, but also that of Secretary for the Congregation of Extraordinary Ecclesiastical Affairs, the group of thirteen cardinals which deals with foreign matters, both ecclesiastical and secular.

In several of these memoranda, addressed personally to Mr. Taylor, Tardini listed in detail the acts of religious persecution being perpetrated at the time in Communist Russia, including the closing down of churches and religious institutions, the deportation, imprisonment and even execution of ecclesiastics, the suppression of Catholic publications and the danger of the spread of Communism generally throughout Europe. One of these, dated September 17, was an excellent summary of opinion in the Vatican which is worthwhile reproducing in view of postwar developments and of the situation in Russia thirty years later:

1. At present Europe is faced with two great dangers: Nazism and Communism. Both are opposed to religion, to Christian civilization, to personal liberty, to peace. At the present moment Nazism is better organized and boasts greater strength.

2. If the war now in progress were to mean the end of both dangers, a period of tranquility would be possible for Europe. But if even one of these two evils, Communism for example, were to remain an active force, Europe would, within a few years, be in a situation identical with that in which it finds itself today. In fact, Communism, once victorious, would find no further resistance in continental Europe and would spread among the Germanic peoples, the Slav races, and finally among the Latins. In consequence, within the space of a few years there would be an enormous Communist bloc, whose inevitable destiny would be to provoke a war with England and America, two countries regarded by the Communists as forming a Capitalist bloc.

3. For the clarification of the above it is well to bear in mind:

   a. that Communism has always profited by the discontent of the people in moments of difficulty. Certainly, with the end of the war, Europe will experience a period of great difficulty and unrest among many Germanic, Slav and Latin peoples.

   b. that Communism is committed not only to a program of expansion through propaganda, but also to a very real and unmistakable program of military aggression. This is proved by the invasion of Poland, Estonia, Finland, Latvia, Lithuania and Bessarabia.

   c. that Communism cannot renounce its struggle against religion and Christian civilization, because it has as its fundamental principle that Capitalism must be destroyed and that religion is but the opium with which Capitalism has drugged the proletariat. Therefore, for the Communists the proposal to destroy "Capitalistic Civilization" is of immediate concern.

   d. that Communism, notwithstanding its pacifist claims, pursues a program which is eminently *militaristic*, a fact which has been demonstrated by the immense war preparations which Communism has made, unknown to all, and which have been revealed in the present Russo-German war.

An excerpt from Tardini's notes recording his meeting with Taylor on September 16 highlights the gap between the Vatican's views on Soviet Russia and those of Roosevelt. Taylor had explained to Tardini that the United States would not allow the Germans to defeat England and would enter the war to avoid this result if necessary. "At this point," Tardini wrote, "I asked

Mr. Taylor for a final explanation. Assuming the survival of communism and the defeat of Nazism, Europe would end up as follows. All the countries (Balkan, Latin, Germanic) would be knocked out. Communism would be triumphant and would permeate all nations. There would thus be within continental Europe an enormous militaristic power (because communism has demonstrated its ability and willingness to arm itself) as aggressive as Nazism (because it is well known that communism tends to overrun everything). Have the United States 'realized' this eventuality? How could they stop it? If unable to do so, would we not therefore be faced, in a few years, by a new enemy, maybe stronger and more dangerous than Hitler? Mr. Taylor seemed surprised by my questions. It seemed almost as though he had never considered the problem. He asked me: 'Do you think so?' 'I am sure of it,' I replied. But Taylor did not pursue the subject."

Following his first audience with the Pope, Taylor informed Ambassador Phillips and his staff at the American Embassy of the contents of Roosevelt's letter on the religious situation in Russia—to their great astonishment, and especially that of Elbridge Durbrow, one of the State Department's leading Soviet specialists. Durbrow, having been stationed in Moscow in 1936, had first-hand knowledge of the question of freedom of religion in the Soviet Union. Knowing from experience how the Communists really felt on the subject, he told Taylor there was little hope that the Soviet government would change its attitude, regardless of what President Roosevelt had written in his letter to the Pope. He added that he could not understand how such a letter as the President's could ever have been written in the first place in view of all the contrary information that was on file in the State Department. The consensus of that particular group was that the President must have either acted alone without previously consulting the Secretary of State, who Durbrow felt certain could not have agreed, or that Roosevelt had concluded that, in spite of all opposition, every means should be employed to encourage the Vatican to lend its moral support to the side of the U.S.S.R. in its struggle against the Nazi aggressor. The latter is undoubtedly the more accurate explanation.

With specific regard to the problem of changing Catholic opinion in the United States, Mr. Taylor asked the Holy Father to request the American hierarchy to inform the faithful that his predecessor, Pius XI, did not in any way mean to condemn the Russian people themselves in his Encyclical "Divini Redemptoris," but only the Soviet Government's attacks on individual liberties.

The Pope's reply to the President's letter, dated September 20, was restricted to generalities, since it was obvious that Roosevelt's optimistic views on the status of religion in Russia were considered grossly exaggerated in the Vatican. In spite of this, Pius XII assured Taylor that he would comply with Roosevelt's request to do at least something to clarify in the minds of American Catholics the terms of the worrisome encyclical. But the Holy Father, in order to maintain his neutral position, was anxious to keep himself and the Holy See out of the limelight. He therefore directed Cardinal Maglione to have Monsignor Tardini sign, in a letter dated September 20, the necessary instructions to the Apostolic Delegate in Washington to contact the American hierarchy on the subject, but only in the strictest confidence in order to insure that neither the Pope nor the Holy See be involved in any way.

Cicognani, realizing the delicacy of the situation, consulted with Archbishop Edward Mooney of Detroit, as well as with Monsignor Ready, the Secretary General of the National Catholic Welfare Conference, before taking any action. They decided that the best way to solve the problem would be the publication of a pastoral letter addressed to the faithful interpreting the Encyclical "Divini Redemptoris" as desired by President Roosevelt. The text of the pastoral letter would then be published in the newspapers. Monsignor John Timothy McNicholas, Archbishop of Cincinnati, was selected for the task, not only because of his personal prestige and his well-known tendency to remain aloof from political questions, but also because of his reputation as an isolationist. Thus there would be no suspicion that the pastoral letter had been the result of outside pressure.

The Apostolic Delegate informed the Vatican on October 28 that "Monsignor McNicholas, after exhorting the faithful to maintain an attitude of Christianity and tolerance when faced with political opinions, recalls the passages in Pius XI's Encyclicals concerning Nazi Germany in which a distinction was made between Nazis and the German people; he then goes on to make the same considerations with respect to the Soviet regime and the Russian people; he then examines the controversial passage in the Encyclical "Divini Redemptoris" (that the faithful should not collaborate in any way with atheistic Communism), placing it in its proper context and drawing the conclusion that it should not be applied to the present moment of armed conflict." The Pastoral letter was published on October 30.

As soon as the text of the letter became known, various archbishops, bishops and Catholic publications in the United States came forward with expressions of affection for the Russian people and pointed out that the policies followed by Washington were not aimed at aiding Communism but only at supporting the Russian people themselves. As further clarification to the hierarchy, the Delegate mentioned to several of them that while it was conceivable, of course, that Communism might gain by such policies, they were still laudable ones and that therefore the evil would have to be taken with the good. Thus Pius XII himself had joined the President in admitting that Hitlerism was an enemy of the Church more dangerous than Stalinism and that the only way to overcome the former was an Allied victory, even if this meant assistance from Soviet Russia.

In addition to the request for the Holy See's favorable interpretation of the Encyclical "Divini Redemptoris," a number of other points were discussed by Mr. Taylor and the Pope:

1. Mr. Taylor briefed the Pope on opinion in the United States regarding the progress of the war. The American people were convinced without exception that Hitler was bound to lose. Although no outright state of war existed between the United States and Germany, preparations for such an event had reached an extraordinary level. There was absolute unanimity in the United States on remaining outside the conflict unless there should be provocation by Hitler or indications that the Allies were destined to be defeated in the end.

2. Mr. Taylor observed that before Italy had entered the war, the Holy See had done everything possible to keep Italy out of it. He then asked Cardinal Maglione whether he thought there was any chance at this stage that Italy might make a separate peace with the Allies. Maglione replied that he saw little hope for this.

3. The Pope expressed concern about the possible bombing of the city of Rome by the Allies or the Germans.

In Mr. Taylor's first audience on September 10, 1941, the Holy Father said that he had been upset by a statement made over the air by a British air marshal on August 24 that the Bomber Command held no false sentiment about the bombing of Rome, and requested Mr. Taylor to try to do something to prevent such action. During the audience of September 16, the Pope gave Mr. Taylor a general warning that the Holy See could not remain silent if any of the basilicas, churches, pontifical buildings or papal institutions were struck during an Allied (at this time British) air raid on Rome. The next day the warning was repeated in writing by Monsignor Tardini in a memorandum left with Taylor.

In reply, Mr. Taylor promised that he would undertake to discourage London (and Washington, should the United States enter the war) from engaging in indiscriminate bombing, and urge that targets be confined to military and communication centers. He suggested that the Vatican should press the Italian Government to warn the Roman population to keep away from these danger zones.

After Mr. and Mrs. Taylor had departed for the United States, I wrote a personal letter to Undersecretary of State Welles stating that in my opinion, as well as in that of my diplomatic colleagues and various Vatican personalities, Mr. Taylor's presence at the Vatican had had a definitely heartening effect upon Pope Pius XII, and that Mr. Taylor's visit had been a success. A copy was forwarded by Welles to Roosevelt, who was pleased to hear from someone on the spot that the trip made by his Personal Representative to the Pope was successful.

In any event, no matter how gloomy the general outlook for religion in Russia was or how exaggerated President Roosevelt's enthusiasm proved to be, Roosevelt was eminently successful in carrying out his plans to assist Russia. On November 7, he was able to declare publicly that Soviet Russia was now eligible for Lend-Lease aid, although there was still much opposition, both Catholic and Protestant, to the idea of helping Communist Russia. Opinion in the United States was becoming more aware of Russia's role in the international conflict and this change of attitude was clearly reflected in October by the rejection by both Houses of Congress of an amendment to the second Lend-Lease Bill forbidding the use of such funds for aid to the Soviet Union.

President Roosevelt's optimistic observations on the religious situation in Russia had now convinced the Vatican that his own intervention on behalf of the Church's interests in that country could be productive. The Holy See, therefore, lost no time in appealing to the President, through Taylor and myself, for help in its charitable endeavors to ease the plight of Roman Catholics in the Soviet Union.

On November 17, the Vatican requested me to ascertain if the United States Government was in a position to inquire in Moscow about the condition of the Poles and Lithuanians deported to Russia and to inform the Holy See of the results. On December 4, the Apostolic Delegate in Washington also asked for the help of the United States Government in caring for hundreds of thousands of these Roman Catholics interned in Russia. I had forwarded to Mr. Taylor a note dated November 1 from the Holy See asking for our intervention to determine the whereabouts and welfare of Monsignor Edward Profittlich, Apostolic Administrator in Estonia, who had been deported by the Soviets. The Department of State replied on December 5:

> It is not believed that any action on the part of the American Government or the American Embassy in Moscow would serve to alleviate Monsignor Profittlich's condition or effect his release, since the Soviet Government has continuously declined to entertain even the most informal representations made to it on behalf of persons in the Soviet Union who are not American citizens. Furthermore, since Monsignor Profittlich is undoubtedly an Estonian citizen, as such he would be considered a Soviet citizen by the government of the U.S.S.R.

The Holy See's expectations ended in disappointment.

It was a discouraging moment, as I felt we were making a little headway in dealing with the Soviet Union on the subject of religion, which was a matter of so much interest both to the Vatican and to the United States. George Kennan was undoubtedly correct when he said in a long memorandum prepared especially for Mr. Taylor on Russian affairs: "Just as in the 15th and 16th centuries, the Czars of Russia fought Roman Catholic influence, not so much out of conviction of dogma as out of fear of foreign influence on a backward and credulous people, so today the present rulers tend to feel that any foreign influence, religious or otherwise, challenges the security of their rule." Nor was the Holy See encouraged by the results of the "crusading spirit" proclaimed from the house tops by the Nazis as they were invading Russia. When I talked with Monsignor Montini in October, he told me that there had been no signs whatsoever of any relaxation of the anti-Christian policies and principles of the Nazis in German-occupied Russia. He was sorry to have to report that just the contrary seemed to be the case. German soldiers, he said, were being instructed by their superiors to follow the rule that "it was not the business of a German to concern himself in any way with religious matters."

On December 7, 1941, the Japanese attacked Pearl Harbor, and a few days later, Italy and Germany declared war against the United States. Before the end of the year, my father moved his office and residence into the Vatican City, where he would spend the next two and a half years.

CHAPTER 3

1942

The Japanese attacked Pearl Harbor on December 7, 1941, and, in view of the Tripartite Pact which they had signed with Germany and Italy on September 27, 1940, it was obvious to the world that the Axis powers would declare war against the United States within the next few days. Eleanor had been with me in Rome for the preceding four months, but as we came to realize that the war would be extended, we decided it prudent for her to rejoin our two children who were still at school in Switzerland. To our dismay, however, the Italian authorities warned us that she would be unable to get an exit visa. Our Embassy telegraphed this disturbing information to Washington on December 9 and requested that the State Department intervene. On the same day the Embassy received a reply saying that the American-born Countess Mary Hammond Roberti, then visiting her parents in the United States, would not be given an exit visa to join her husband, Count Guerino Roberti, at the Italian Embassy in Mexico City unless the Italian exit visa for my wife were issued.

As I recall, our spirits were pretty low as we contemplated the possibility of Eleanor's not joining our children, as well as the possibility that the Robertis, friends of ours, might also be separated for an indefinite period. Fortunately, the Eternal City was still able to provide cheerful diversion even at this low ebb in our morale. My wife and I went to the Rome Opera and greatly enjoyed the double-billed comedies, *Gianni Schicchi* by Puccini and *Le Coq d'Or* by Rimski-Korsakov.

The next day Eleanor and I proceeded to the Vatican to explain our troubles to Monsignor Montini, and requested his intervention on Eleanor's behalf. Monsignor Montini agreed to get in touch with Marchese Blasco Lanza d'Ayeta, one of the more important figures of the Foreign Office, who was the godson of the American wife of Sumner Welles. Upon returning to the hotel, we were informed that d'Ayeta was ready to receive us immediately at the Foreign Office in the Palazzo Chigi. There he assured us that everything had been arranged for Eleanor to go to Switzerland whenever it was convenient for her to leave. I wired the Department on December 10 that my wife had been granted an exit visa solely on the ground that she was the wife of a diplomat accredited to the Holy See. Whether the Roberti issue influenced the change of heart in the Italian Foreign Office is difficult to say, as the subject was never mentioned in any of our conversations. In any event, Eleanor was now free to make her plans for departure.

Meanwhile momentous happenings were taking place in Rome. On December 12, five days after Pearl Harbor, Mussolini stood on his famous balcony overlooking the Piazza Venezia to address a vast sea of upturned faces and declared war on the United States. He wore his full dress military uniform and his face displayed a satisfied smile. He knew that at precisely the same hour, 2:50 P.M, Hitler would be standing before the Reichstag in Berlin to make the same declaration.

Twenty minutes before Mussolini began speaking from his balcony, the Italian Foreign Minister had called George Wadsworth, our Chargé d'Affaires to the Italian Government, into his office to inform him that the King of Italy had already declared his country to be at war against the United States. The next day, on December 13, the United States in turn declared war on both Italy and Germany. For the first time in history, Italians and Americans were facing each other in hostile camps.

It was now impossible for me to continue to maintain an office and residence on Italian soil. I had two choices: I could either move to a neutral territory, such as the Vatican City or Switzerland, or I could return to the United States with the Embassy staff on the diplomatic train which would eventually leave Italy. The uncertainty did not last long. I received a telegram from Washington, the last one that our Embassy itself handled, informing me that it was assumed in the State Department that I would be moving immediately into the Vatican City. The next day I answered through the Swiss Minister in Rome (Switzerland had by then taken over the affairs of the United States) that I would follow the Department's instructions without hesitation, although some questions had arisen between the Vatican and the Italian Government regarding my diplomatic status.

Arrangements for my wife's departure for Switzerland had, with difficulty, finally been cleared with the Italian authorities. It was a relief to know that she would be able to leave, even though it was on the very day that war was declared by the United States against Italy. Under these foreboding circumstances, little incidents of her voyage naturally stood out in bold relief. She boarded the train alone at Rome Central Station in a complete blackout, as I was not allowed by the Italian Police to see her off. She felt agitated and nervous, and sleep was out of the question. It was four o'clock in the morning when she descended from her sleeping car into the wintry, cavernous darkness of the Milan railway station to await the departure of her connecting train for Domodossola on the Swiss frontier. As she stepped down onto the station platform she saw that a man was obviously waiting for her. Introductions were hardly necessary as it was easy to grasp that he was the Italian secret service agent assigned to her. Eleanor sought to make the best of this unenviable situation and invited her escort to share the "instant" Nescafé she always carried with her in her handbag on her trips back and forth from Switzerland. Together they found the necessary steaming hot water in the bar of the station and enjoyed the cheer that the beverage produced in the bleak early morning hours. The escort seemed especially pleased, since the war shortages in Italy made it practically impossible for him to enjoy the luxury of pure, unadulterated coffee, albeit the powdered kind.

At noon, her train from Milan reached the frontier, where the Italian border guards and customs inspectors entered her compartment, making the usual enquiries whether the passengers had anything to declare. When Eleanor's turn came, she firmly answered "no." However, pressed further as to whether she was carrying any foreign currency, she admitted she had the same two hundred dollars in Swiss francs which she had brought with her when entering Italy several months before. Bearing a diplomatic passport, she had not been required to fill out the form she would need to present on leaving. The customs inspector kept demanding that she give up the cash since she was unable to produce an exit certificate. But she flatly refused, insisting that hers was a diplomatic passport and for that reason she was not obliged to do so. Finally the inspector implored, "But Signora, don't you realize that we are now at war with each other and because of that your diplomatic passport has lost all its meaning?" She replied, with her Texas stubbornness coming to the fore, "Yes, I know all that, but it's my money and you have no right to take it from me, war or no war!" Thereupon the inspector gave up the struggle and, with a characteristic

Italian shrug and sigh, simply murmured *eh, va bene*, before
retreating to his next victims in a nearby compartment. My wife,
with her Swiss francs safely in hand, could pause to reflect once
more on how "simpatico" Italians really were, no matter what
the circumstances might be.

Another example of the "simpatico" character of the Italian
people had been shown by an event which occurred the day
before Italy declared war on the United States. In July of 1937, I
had been awarded an important decoration, Commander of the
Order of the Crown of Italy, by the King of Italy and Emperor
of Ethiopia, in recognition of my work during the eleven years
that I had been on the staff of the American Embassy in Rome.
Under U.S. State Department regulations, I was obliged at the
time to refuse the honor. Four years later, at this fateful moment
in Italo-American history, one of my friends at the Protocol Section of the Foreign Office, Signor Mario Panza, met me in the
lobby of the Excelsior Hotel, where he and his American wife
were also living. Without a word, he handed me the decoration
and accompanying citation which had been stowed away in his
office ever since I had been unable to accept it. No explanation
was forthcoming for his action, as my friend dared not talk to
me in public. However, I was so affected by the warm sentiments he conveyed to me through the expressions on his face
and his understanding smile that I could not refuse the offer
again, even though I never expected to have an opportunity to
wear the decoration, especially since Italy was now an enemy of
the United States.

After Eleanor's return to Switzerland, I was now left alone
in the Excelsior Hotel. In spite of the instructions from Washington, the course I should follow remained unclear. On the day
that Italy declared war on the United States, the Italian Ambassador to the Holy See, Bernardo Attolico, made a special visit to

the Cardinal Secretary of State to inform the latter that the Government of Italy considered it doubtful that I could be regarded as possessing diplomatic status and consequent immunity while on Italian soil. He pointed out that according to the official record, I was the "Assistant" to the "Personal Representative of the President of the United States," who, in turn, had never been and was not then a representative of the United States but only of the President. Furthermore, he noted that President Roosevelt had stated publicly several times that no formal diplomatic relations existed between his country and the Holy See, and that the Personal Representative was himself absent from Italy, rendering the status of his "Assistant" even more ambiguous.

That evening I was called to the Vatican and informed of the views of the Italian Ambassador; I had the impression that the Vatican had taken them seriously. The Italian Government, it seemed, was preparing to challenge my right to take up residence in the Vatican City because of my admittedly doubtful diplomatic status. Since my diplomatic immunity might also be questioned, my personal liberty on Italian soil could well be restricted. The archives in my office at the Excelsior Hotel now seemed to be in danger of confiscation, and as our Embassy urged me to send them into the Vatican City for safekeeping, their transfer was immediately arranged.

On the following day, December 12, the Vatican offered me its own channels of communication through the Secretariat of State and the Apostolic Delegate in Washington. Accepting the offer, I sent a telegram to the Department giving a résumé of Signor Attolico's warnings, and suggesting that, in order to avoid further complications, my diplomatic status should be regularized as soon as possible by appointing me either a Minister or a Chargé d'Affaires of the United States to the Holy See. I added that I hoped the President would devise some formula under which he could act without delay, even though the appointment might only be for the duration of the war.

Although I was disappointed not to receive immediate authorization from Washington to change my status, I was nevertheless somewhat relieved on December 13 when I was advised by the Swiss Legation, now in charge of American affairs, that insofar as the Italian Foreign Office was concerned there was no objection to the change of residence from the Excelsior Hotel to the Vatican City for myself and my American secretary. This information was diametrically opposed to the reports I kept receiving from Vatican sources. In fact, the rumor that I might not be allowed to move into the Vatican was causing considerable concern among my diplomatic colleagues inside the Vatican walls. D'Arcy Osborne, the British Minister, went to see the Cardinal Secretary of State to protest against any delay in my transfer, expressing the hope that my case would not turn into another Mirosevic scandal, further harming the reputation of the Holy See.

In the meantime, residing on enemy territory was becoming increasingly unpleasant for me. During the five days I spent at the Excelsior Hotel after war had been declared, I was allowed reasonable liberty of movement by the Italian authorities. Nevertheless, the attitude of the hotel staff became more suspicious and hostile than ever, as did that of my Italian friends staying at the hotel. In addition, both my American secretary, Miss Flammia, and I were receiving a series of anonymous and disturbing telephone calls, threatening us with violence should we attempt to leave the premises of the hotel. I decided, therefore, to move immediately into the Vatican City, even though there was a good chance of my being arrested by the Italian police along the way. Once inside the Pope's domain, it would be obviously more difficult for the Italians to get rid of me.

I informed the Holy See on Monday, December 15, 1941, of my desire to move into the Vatican without further delay, and surprisingly enough it was accepted without comment. Nor did the Italian Foreign Office, again to my surprise, offer any objection when it was notified by the Holy See of my intended action. On the following afternoon I loaded my car with my personal belongings in front of the Excelsior Hotel and then drove across the River Tiber to the Vatican City, where I was courteously, if not enthusiastically, received by my Vatican hosts. I would not set foot again in Rome for the next two and one half years.

The era of my confinement had begun. I used the facilities of the Vatican Secretariat of State to announce to the State Department that I had arrived safely inside the Vatican City and that I had received assurances that my future communication with Washington would be maintained through the Vatican pouches by way of Switzerland as long as that country remained free. I once more insisted upon the desirability of having my diplomatic status defined. But back in Washington the wheels of government ground slowly. On December 13, the Apostolic Delegate addressed a memorandum to Secretary of State Cordell Hull informing him that the Italian Government opposed the Vatican's receiving an American representative inside the Vatican City, but that the Holy See would not yield to this pressure. Cicognani assured the State Department that if I were appointed Minister or Chargé d'Affaires to the Holy See, the Vatican would not expect reciprocity by converting the Delegation in Washington to a Nunciature, which would have meant the establishment of formal diplomatic relations between the United States and the Holy See.

On December 17, Mr. Taylor informed President Roosevelt that I had already moved into the Vatican City. On the same day, Sumner Welles sent the following letter to the President:

Dear Mr President:

I am enclosing for your information a copy of a memorandum I have received from the Apostolic Delegate.

In this memorandum Archbishop Cicognani indicates that the Italian Government may raise strong objection to the continued residence of Tittmann in the Vatican City unless Tittmann receives some official status such as Chargé d'Affaires. The Secretary (Cordell Hull) agrees with me that it is of very great importance that Tittmann remain in the Vatican City so that we may continue contact through him with the Holy See. If we ascertain that the Vatican will have to give in to Italian pressure and agree to have Tittmann leave, it seems to me that you will wish to consider favorably Tittmann's designation as Chargé d'Affaires in order to avoid this result.

Will you let me know if the Department has your authorization to confer the rank of Chargé d'Affaires upon Tittmann should we have word that it is absolutely necessary in order to avoid his departure?

Believe me, Faithfully yours,

Sumner Welles (Under Secretary of State)

Shortly thereafter, the letter was returned to Welles with the initials "SW OK FDR" inscribed in the President's own hand on the top of the first page, and I was informed that the President had authorized me the rank of Chargé d'Affaires.

At a routine year-end private audience I had with the Holy Father on December 29, 1941, he mentioned that he was very glad indeed that my diplomatic status had now been clarified, since recently the Italian Ambassador to the Holy See, Attolico, had been asking some pointed questions in my regard which made it prudent to clear the matter without delay. I told the

Pope that I considered the threatening attitude of Ambassador Attolico rather strange and I asked the Holy Father whether Attolico might not have been influenced by the Secret Police. In reply to my remark, the Holy Father merely stated that he assumed that the Ambassador took his orders from the Ministry of Foreign Affairs and from no one else. I gathered that the Pope was not ready to reveal, if indeed he understood, what was behind the mysterious démarche.

When Attolico had been in Berlin, he had been struck by Hitler's open antagonism towards the Holy See in general and in particular by the Fuehrer's intense disapproval of Allied diplomats inside the Vatican City, a group which he frequently branded "a nest of spies." Attolico was also aware that Hitler was continually seeking some excuse on which to base a formal demand by the Axis that the diplomats be expelled from the Vatican City. Attolico feared that the desired pretext could easily be forthcoming were the Holy See to increase the number of "spies" by adding an American official, who was not even a diplomat, to the "nest." Under the circumstances, the Italian Ambassador undoubtedly sensed that it would be wiser for me to stay out of the Vatican City altogether. But if this were impossible, then I should at least be given normal diplomatic status before I went in, which would considerably reduce the effectiveness of the argument that Hitler might raise for hostile action against the Allied diplomats. Obviously, the Holy See shared Attolico's apprehensions and was for this reason anxious to resolve the question.

In retrospect, I believe that there had been some sort of "combinazione" (personal understanding) between Attolico and certain Vatican officials in order to guard against Hitler's possible designs. The ejection of the diplomats would have been a serious blow to the provisions of the Lateran Treaty between Italy and the Holy See, thus damaging not only the interests of

the Holy See but those of Italy as well. Attolico surely conduct-
ed himself in the best possible manner in the interests of his
country, but unfortunately, within a few weeks, he died suddenly from a liver complaint with heart complications.

For a while, my colleagues in the Vatican City wondered
whether the American mission was to be regarded as an embassy
or a legation, most of them believing that it would most certainly be an embassy since Mr. Taylor held the rank of Ambassador.
In any event, they and everyone else in the Vatican and even in
Rome considered as an accomplished and desirable fact that formal diplomatic relations between the United States and the Holy
See had now been established. I personally questioned this interpretation, since I continued to feel that anti-Catholic feeling at
home could not be fully overcome even though we were now at
war. In order to clarify matters and put an end to fruitless con-
jectures, I queried the State Department on January 9, 1942:

> Now that I have been given the rank of Chargé
> d'Affaires to the Holy See, the question arises as to whether
> this mission is to be considered a legation or an embassy. I
> have had frequent inquiries with respect to this point and
> I am frankly at a loss for an intelligible reply.

The Department replied:

> In accordance with Section 24 of the Act of February
> 23, 1931 you have been designated to act as Chargé d'Af-
> faires. If enquiries are made, you may explain that you
> are temporarily acting in that capacity while the Presi-
> dent's Special Representative is absent.

No mention was made in any of the State Department's messages of an embassy or legation and the words "Holy See" were

avoided, a cautious attitude on the part of Washington I had
expected.

Naturally, none of this shadowy language was understood,
either by my colleagues or anyone on the Vatican staff, unless
they had been aware of the confusing details of Myron Taylor's
appointment two years previously. Be that as it may, in the eyes
of the Italian Government and of almost everyone else in Rome,
there was no doubt that from then on I was the Chargé d'Affaires of the United States to the Holy See in every sense of the
word, and that was all there was to it.

The Italian Government identity cards, which diplomats
accredited to the Holy See were required to carry with them
and which were delivered through the Secretariat of State, were
not received by myself and my wife until June 1942, six months
after I had entered the Vatican City and one year after I had
been assigned to the Holy See. The Italian identity cards were
back-dated to December 1, 1941, in order to indicate that they
had been issued before we had become enemies of Italy. On my
Italian card I was referred to as "Attaché and Chargé d'Affaires
of the United States Embassy near the Holy See." The receipt of
these official documents further helped to set our minds at rest,
at least as regards the Italian Government.

I entered my new home in the Vatican City on December 16,
1941. The apartment designated for me and my family was on
the second of two floors of the "palazzino" or annex of Santa
Marta. It was a long rambling affair with twelve rooms. There
was a spacious living room, a dining room, and a kitchen, which
were completely separated from three large bedrooms, one with
an adjoining bathroom, and two smaller rooms. Servants' quarters were in the rear at the end of a long corridor which bridged
a passageway below. The living room and dining room were the
largest in Santa Marta and had been used as dormitories for

groups of pilgrims, whereas the accommodations for pilgrims in the main building were mostly cells for individuals.

In addition, the apartment had a small private garden terrace. Although diminutive, it was conveniently located adjoining our living room. Begonias, the omnipresent flowers in the Vatican gardens, grew along the borders of our terrace, and in the middle was a small boxwood parterre. A little peach tree stood nearby, which produced tiny inedible fruit and gave no shade. With the assistance of a Vatican gardener, we planted tomatoes and other vegetables, with little success. We originally had hoped to eat on the terrace "al fresco," but with the warmer weather came those barely visible biting insects known in the Venetian vernacular as "pappataci" or "silent eaters," and they with the ants discouraged this plan.

At the time I moved in, the apartment was completely bare except for the large bedrooms and the bathroom which were adequately furnished, but occupied by Monsignor Carlo Emanuele Toraldo. He was a member of the "Pope's Family," with the puzzling title of "Privy Chamberlain Participating" under the subheading "Keeper of the Wardrobe," or the guardian of the Pontiff's robes. Toraldo was obviously an important Vatican personality and it was difficult for me to hasten his departure simply for myself alone, though my family was due to arrive shortly. The Monsignor took three months to move out.

In the meantime I occupied the two small rooms at the head of the stairway, using one for my office and one for my bedroom. But I was obliged to walk over that never-ending bridge to reach the only bathroom available to me, back in the servants' quarters. It was no fun to make the voyage on a cold wintry night, especially since there was no heating of any kind. Had it not been for the kind attentions of D'Arcy Osborne's warmhearted and resourceful butler, John May, I would have felt completely lost and discouraged in those dreary and uncomfortable surroundings. John was able to procure a bed, linen, several wooden chairs, and a few kitchen utensils with which I could prepare breakfast.

I was not yet in a position to take on a domestic household. So if I was not invited elsewhere, I arranged to have lunch, paying my own way, with D'Arcy Osborne in his apartment on the top floor of the main building and to have dinner in the same way with the Secretary of the Yugoslav Legation, Kosta Zukic, and his wife Betsa, who lived below me on the ground floor. Had I desired to do so, I could have taken my meals regularly in the refectory of the hospice administered by the nuns. They provided excellent food for the convenience of the monsignors and diplomats in Santa Marta, but it seemed more fun to eat with my friends.

Personal and unofficial communication facilities with the outside world were difficult for the diplomats inside the Vatican. I had received no word from my family or friends in the United States for the past month. In fact, the first letter I was to receive from my mother in Saint Louis did not arrive until the middle of March. The correspondence was held up by the Italian censors and only released at the urgent request of the Vatican. I did, however, receive regular letters from my wife and sons in Switzerland through the Vatican diplomatic courier from Bern.

I was finding confinement in the Vatican City not nearly as difficult as it would have seemed. I had almost daily contact with the officials of the Secretariat of State and with Engineer Galeazzi, Director General of the Technical Services of the State of the Vatican City, on purely administrative and household matters. He was, in fact, the uncrowned governor of the Vatican State, although another layman, Marchese Camilo Serafino, officially held that title. An architect by profession, Galeazzi wielded great influence, not only because he seemed to be more or less responsible for the everyday living conditions for those residing within the Vatican City, but also because of his close personal relationship with the Pope. As far as we diplomats were concerned, Galeazzi was indeed our "housekeeper," and it was difficult to imagine getting along without his counsel and assistance. I often called on him in his office in the impressive new Governatorato building located halfway up the hill leading to the gardens, to discuss the scarcity of food or gasoline. Galeazzi had his workmen construct an open-hearth fireplace in our living room to keep us warm when the central heating proved inadequate. He sometimes was able to provide us, especially when we had guests as an excuse, the occasional bottle of Cognac, French champagne, or even Scotch whisky. Ordinary Italian wines were always available at the Vatican food mart.

There was enough work in my new location to keep me busy with the same office hours as I had maintained in Rome. There would always be visitors from the outside, bringing in the latest news and seeking advice. In this way, until their departure in May, I kept in close touch with our Embassy staff in Rome. I had to prepare bi-weekly reports as the Vatican pouch left for Bern on Tuesdays and Fridays.

My American secretary, Miss Nicolina Flammia, remained at the Excelsior Hotel during the first six months that I was in Santa Marta, undecided whether to stay with me, permanently shut in the Vatican, or whether to return to the United States with the Rome Embassy staff. Miss Flammia finally chose to stay, much to my relief. In the meantime, with special permission from the Italian Foreign Office, she acted as my liaison officer with the American Embassy in Rome, being driven back and forth every day by my chauffeur, Umberto. She always brought me the latest news as well as some serviceable object picked up "by chance" at the Embassy chancery.

My father's memoirs contain only a few references to his secretary, Miss Flammia, during her stay in the Vatican. Yet she was part of our household, since she occupied one of the smaller rooms in the Santa Marta apartment and, if I remember correctly, shared her meals with us. She was a relatively young woman, probably in her early thirties, and I believe she must have been an efficient secretary. She gave me typing lessons in her spare time during the 1942 summer holidays. Relations between her and my father gradually deteriorated, however. The unavailability of a normal social life within the Vatican no doubt got on her nerves, and, being a headstrong woman, she became irritable and even insubordinate at times. Her language was colorful: When the Vatican authorities were slow in providing some facility, she would urge my father to "put the screws on Montini." She did not approve of the Italians referring to my father as "excellency," and would address testy notes to him when she felt that he was not sufficiently displaying his patriotism. She asked for a transfer (or perhaps my father insisted on it) during the first half of 1943 and was replaced by another State Department clerk, Miss Christener, a middle-aged spinster who seemed better able to cope with the Vatican environment. Unfortunately there is no record in my father's papers as to how these personnel changes were effected, as they must have been unusually complicated, given the wartime conditions. They were another example of the "flexible" attitude of the Italian authorities.

I did not have a confidential code in the Vatican, but its lack was of no great importance, since Allied diplomats were not permitted to send messages in cipher via the Vatican Radio or Telegraph Office under any circumstances. The procedure I used for sending messages home was the same which my colleagues had been using for over a year. An envelope containing confidential telegrams and written reports would be taken to the Secretariat of State twice a week for forwarding to the American

Minister in Bern via the Nunciature. The Bern Legation staff would then code the telegrams and send them off to Washington either by cable or radio. Written reports would be forwarded by mail or courier. Coming back, confidential instructions from Washington were telegraphed to the Legation in Bern where they would be decoded and forwarded to me in clear via the Nuncio's diplomatic pouch to the Secretariat of State. Written correspondence was routed the same way. On rare occasions my correspondence traveled via the Nuncio in Lisbon in both directions.

I sent 663 telegrams during my two and one half year stay in the Vatican. It took an average of seven days for each to reach its destination. After the German occupation of Rome in September 1943, it often took much longer. I also forwarded 299 written reports, and these took one month or even two to arrive in Washington. The person who usually carried the Vatican pouch bearing my correspondence both ways between the Vatican City and Bern was most often the official courier of the Swiss Legation in Rome. Sometimes it was a Monsignor who happened to be traveling to Switzerland. Even though my correspondence was entrusted to reliable neutral authorities, I was never absolutely certain that the Germans or the Italians could not secretly examine my messages. The same apprehension existed in the State Department at home, and was the main reason why I was never supplied with a secret code. Several times I asked for one, because it often seemed wiser to code confidential telegrams in my own office. But Washington felt that no safe means was available to get such a code to me. However, no instance of any violation of the Vatican pouch bearing my messages was ever brought to my attention.

The financing of the American mission in the Vatican was the subject of a special agreement with the Holy See. The currency we lived with was the Italian lira. Remittances to the Holy See of American dollars by way of a neutral country like Switzerland were discouraged by the United States, as there was a possibility that the monies could fall into Italian hands. The Holy See therefore agreed to furnish me each month, against dollars deposited by the State Department in the Morgan Bank in New York to the credit of the Vatican Finance Office, with 28,500 lire, equivalent to 1500 dollars. The exchange rate, 19 lire to the dollar, was in effect on the day war was declared; it was applied by the Vatican during my entire sojourn there, even though the "black market" rate in Rome rose to over five times as many lire to the dollar. I was not permitted by my government to take advantage of the black market rate, to avoid our currency from falling into enemy hands.

The monthly 28,500 lire covered the salaries and allowances for myself and my secretary. Diplomats were charged no rent for apartments in Santa Marta, as we were considered guests of the Holy Father, but we had to pay for utilities. There was also a charge of 100 lire (5 dollars) every six months for the telephone, although no calls were permitted outside the Vatican walls. Garage space for the automobile cost 50 lire per month. The nuns expected a modest donation from each diplomat of about 1000 lire (about 50 dollars) three times a year in order to help cover administrative costs for Santa Marta. Food prices were at first extremely low, since we were allowed to purchase from the Vatican market. We also had the unusual privilege of buying fresh milk, cream, eggs, vegetables, and fruits in season such as the delicious Nemi strawberries, from the Pope's farm at Castelgandolfo in the Alban Hills. However, as the war progressed, prices for those inside the Vatican increased considerably. The Vatican authorities, sensitive to the rising cost of living elsewhere in Italy, did not feel it fair for a few Vatican residents to enjoy cheap provisioning.

During my stay in the Vatican City, I was received, as were other chiefs-of-mission, by the Cardinal Secretary of State. Before his appointment to that position by Pope Pius XII, His Eminence Luigi Cardinal Maglione had been a career diplomat who had spent some time as the Vatican's representative and Apostolic Nuncio in Switzerland. In 1926, he was transferred to the Nunciature in Paris, where he remained for ten years. Just as the Allies were apt to regard Pius XII as pro-German because of his extended sojourn in Munich and Berlin, so the Axis often branded his Secretary of State as being pro-French because of his many years in Paris. Cardinal Maglione, a distinguished and strong-minded man, was much older than me, and our relationship remained formal, as it had to be. Yet he was a likeable, soft-spoken individual, with a great sense of humor; he was well-known for his distinctive chuckle. In his antechamber I was likely to find myself in close proximity to representatives of enemy countries.

On Fridays, I conferred with the Undersecretaries, Monsignor Domenico Tardini and Monsignor Giovanni Battista Montini. Tardini, a handsome man with a blunt manner and a wry sense of humor, handled political matters, while Montini, courteous and aristocratic, dealt with the diplomatic affairs, but in practice they were both involved in all of the Vatican's international affairs. I saw more of Montini than Tardini, as I felt that he had a closer relationship with the Pope and thus could better reflect the views of the Holy Father.

My family planned to arrive in the Vatican City from Switzerland on March 22, 1942. I was concerned by the slow progress on Monsignor Toraldo's new apartment, however, and I even went so far as to write to Monsignor Montini requesting that Toraldo release some of his rooms for the arrival of my family. I even suggested that he perhaps could share his bathroom with us and it may have been this thought which precipitated some action. The monsignor moved out almost immediately.

Early in the war we had learned that the Italian Government was not inclined to accept the liberal interpretation that the Vatican wished to place on certain of the Lateran Treaty provisions concerning the Allied diplomats accredited to the Holy See. But we had been pleased with the way the Vatican, by exercising its sovereignty under the treaty, had successfully persuaded the Italian Government to allow our two sons, aged 10 and 13, to spend their Easter, summer, and Christmas vacations from the Rosey School in Switzerland with us in the Vatican. Since they were too young to travel alone through enemy territory, they were accompanied by their Swiss governess, Jane Morerod. At the Swiss-Italian border, an Italian secret police agent boarded the train to stand guard outside their sleeping compartment during the 16-hour journey on to Rome. The agent was always the same, and he became their friend; once in Rome, he escorted them in a taxi to the Vatican gates, depositing them safely and giving them a warm farewell.

The imminent arrival of my family inspired me to complete my household, which at first only consisted of Umberto, my chauffeur. I hired a couple named Fani and Velia, who had been butler and maid for Ambassador Phillips at the Embassy, and Ianni, a Greek chef specializing in Middle East dishes. When food became scarce, Ianni always produced, wearing his white chef's hat, delicious meals from practically nothing. He was very strict with us, saving provisions and never allowing us to splurge. When things got really bad, he would leave Rome on the train and walk for miles in the country to bring back fresh vegetables grown by his farmer friends. Ianni, his wife, and his daughter lived in Rome. Fani and Velia moved into Santa Marta with their five-year-old daughter, who very tragically died on

Christmas Day two years later. It worked perfectly, though the combination of nationalities was unusual. The Italian butler and maid were our enemies, while the Greek was our friend, but an enemy of the Italians. Occasionally Ianni's wife would sense the Italian police casing their apartment in Rome, so Ianni would install a temporary cot in our kitchen for a week or so until the crisis passed.

Our new domestics were happy to be in the Vatican, especially as provisions were very scarce outside. They were helpful and loyal throughout our stay, although the possibility of espionage by Italians employed by Allied diplomats was always on our minds. Doubtless each Italian had been instructed to report any intelligence picked up in the Vatican. But I was aware of only one instance among my colleagues where this took place. Luigi, D'Arcy Osborne's Italian butler, removed the British Legation's secret code during one or two nights to have it photographed before bringing it back.

Although I never went into Rome during our stay in the Vatican, my wife obtained permission, before the situation in Rome became more difficult, to visit a dentist and her hairdresser in Rome on several occasions. On these outings she was naturally accompanied by an Italian secret service man. Once at the hairdresser she encountered by chance one of her good friends from Rome, and they were able to arrange a secret rendezvous among the Egyptian mummies in the Vatican museum.

On the other hand, various tradesmen and professionals were allowed into the Vatican City to administer to our needs. I recall a barber came at regular intervals to my office, and a manicurist came in several times a month, and once continued her manicuring unperturbed right through a rather severe air raid, even as Eleanor's hands turned to icicles with fright. D'Arcy Osborne, who had vowed never again to have to request permission of the Italian authorities to go into Rome, once brought into his apartment a dentist with his special chair and other paraphernalia, and a number of people made appointments to see him. We also had a tailor come in who made us several suits.

Furnishings for our empty apartment soon began to arrive from all directions. From the American Embassy Chancery and residence in Rome came supplies for the office, comfortable chairs for the living room, government china and glassware, and a large moving-picture projector which proved to be the only one available to diplomats within the Vatican. From the homes of Americans permitted to stay temporarily in Rome, and from American-born wives of Italians, we received flat silver, linen, oil paintings, rugs, an entire library, and even a grand piano. They were, of course, very kind in helping us out, but for them too it was useful as the Vatican City was a safe haven for their possessions. The Vatican itself provided heavy dark blue curtains for all of the windows in the apartment to keep light from being visible outside at night; blackout regulations were in effect in the Vatican as well as in Rome.

There were daily tennis games at the Abyssinian College tennis court located in a far corner of the Vatican gardens—the only sport activity available inside the Vatican. Fortunately, the Italian authorities permitted the diplomatic families residing in the Vatican to drive to the sea at Fregene twice a week during hot weather. Fregene was a village about 35 kilometers from Rome with a beautiful beach and an extensive pine forest. The automobiles of the enemy diplomats did not have to pass through Rome itself—the Italians would not have permitted this—since the road to Fregene was the Via Aurelia which began just outside our walls and led immediately to the countryside.

During this first summer, I joined my family several times on their Tuesday and Thursday expeditions to the sea. On the day prior to the outings, we would notify the Secretariat of State so that an Italian police escort could be arranged. Our Buick would be loaded with picnic baskets and beach equipment, and in St. Peter's Square a Rome police officer would join us, sitting in the front seat next to Umberto, our chauffeur, and usually dozing off. Once in Fregene, those two would go to a restaurant to have lunch and drink wine, while we proceeded to the beach for our picnic and swim. Later in the afternoon, we would pick up Umberto and the policeman, who were often feeling very mellow; once I recall it seemed advisable to place them in the back seat and do the driving ourselves. On the way home, we would purchase fresh vegetables, including corn, from roadside vegetable stands.

One Fregene outing ended in an embarrassing incident for the diplomats and the Holy See. The two attractive teenage daughters of the Peruvian ambassador, upon their return from the beach to their apartment in the Vatican, proceeded to wash the sand out of their hair. Dressed in negligées, they chose the only window with sun in which to dry their hair, little realizing that they could be seen clearly from the offices of Cardinal Canali, President of the Governing Board of the Vatican City State. The Cardinal was obliged to pull down his shades to hide the view from the monsignore working in his office. He sent a formal complaint to the ambassador, many apologies were forthcoming, and this unusual spectacle was never repeated.

Luckily for us, the Pope's gardens formed a hilly park, Mons Vaticanus, behind the great Basilica of St. Peter, covering more than fifty acres, or about one half of the whole area of the Vatican City State. Spread throughout the gardens were more than forty fountains of varying sizes and artistic merit, many with white water lilies floating in their mossy-rimmed pools. The gardens were beautifully landscaped with pleasant stone-paved paths climbing up the steep slopes leading to passageways under arching ilex trees. The shrubberies of fragrant bay, the cedars and the cypresses, palm trees and oleanders, graceful eucalyptus and noble umbrella pines all contributed to the semi-tropical atmosphere of the gardens. Begonias, camellias, gardenias, and roses bloomed in season and were often gathered by the ladies of Santa Marta to decorate their salons. But it was not only the trees, flowers, and fountains that made the Vatican Gardens so attractive, but also the variety of vistas revealing the architectural wonders at the foot of the hill. As I gazed in awe at St. Peter's with its dome and Sistine Chapel, both of which stood out beautifully from many vantage points, I felt that the cage in which we were all living was indeed a gilded one.

One of the consequences of living in the Vatican City was, of course, that of being close to the Holy Father. The occasions on which I was received privately by the Holy Father were rare, perhaps once every four months during my two and one half year stay; a few times I was invited to bring along my wife and two sons. But we saw the Pontiff at the great public functions in St. Peter's and in the Sistine Chapel, and particularly when he invited the diplomats to his Christmas Eve midnight masses in his private Matilda Chapel.

Sometimes, if we were lucky, we would see him in his automobile being driven up to the Vatican Gardens where he would stroll back and forth along the covered walk reading his breviary or the manuscript of an address he was preparing. The Gardens were reserved exclusively for his use between the hours of three and five in the afternoon. If anyone else lingered there too long, the Vatican gendarmes would hustle them out.

The Pope's outstanding characteristic was his physical charm. The finely chiseled head and features, with his flashing black eyes magnified under his glasses, reminded one of Savonarola. His expression in repose was ascetic, but when animated it immediately became humane and smiling. His frame was tall and spare and his movements well coordinated and graceful. This pleasing impression was enhanced by an impeccably tailored soutane which seemed to flow along in rhythm as he moved. His hands, with their long, shapely fingers, were of great beauty and he did not hesitate to make effective use of them when talking. He was conscious of his personal charm and knew how to exploit it.

He was an excellent linguist, fluent in German, French, and, of course, Italian, possessing a working knowledge of many other foreign languages as well. He did not, however, feel at home in English, although it amused him to give the impression that he was also master of that tongue. I remember that whenever the Pope and I conversed together, he would always start out speaking English, but would gradually change to his native Italian with a smile and a distinct sigh of relief.

Pope Pius XII also had a sense of humor. During the winter months of 1943 and 1944, Rome was without available heating fuels of any kind, which meant that the population suffered from the cold. Since the Supreme Pontiff was also the Archbishop and Metropolitan of the Province of Rome as well as the Sovereign of the Vatican City State, he felt that it was only fair that his Vatican citizens should undergo the same privations as the faithful in the Diocese. Accordingly, he decreed that there should be no heating of any Vatican City apartments or offices, not even with the enormous pile of coal which lay well hidden in the Vatican Gardens. One cold morning in February 1943, I went to see the Pope on official business in his unheated library. On previous occasions, he always met me at the door to shake hands and then accompanied me back to his desk where we would both be seated. But this time when I appeared, the Pope did not rise from his chair, but instead waved me in and pointed to the empty seat next to him for my use. Before our conversation began, he quickly pulled off a woolen blanket which I had noticed around his knees and revealed an oversized hot water bag lying in his lap. Smiling, he explained, "Now you understand why I could not get up to greet you at the door. My German housekeeper, Mother Pasqualina, in one of her more ferocious moments, sent it by messenger from my apartment to me here with instructions that I should keep it on my knees during the working hours at my desk in order to prevent me from catching cold. An exaggeration, no doubt, but what else could I do? After all, 'c'est la guerre.'"

The Bavarian-born Mother Pasqualina Lehnert of the Franciscan Order of the Sister Teachers of the Holy Cross (Gray Nuns of St. Gall, Switzerland), with two other German nuns from the same order, managed the household affairs in the Pope's private apartment. They assured the supply of food and other necessities of life, a job which became increasingly difficult as supplies became more scarce. Mother Lehnert was often seen riding both in and out of the Vatican City, in the back seat of the Pope's official limousine, on one of her shopping tours.

Although it may be assumed that the Pope had the last word in everything, there was nevertheless ample evidence that he was always careful to seek what he considered the best advice before taking action. With his diplomatic background, he was inclined to see both sides of a question, and this may have given others the impression that he was sometimes timid and reluctant to make decisions, especially in foreign affairs. In reality this was not the case. He was, in fact, decisive and even autocratic in his handling of foreign relations. He insisted on keeping all the reins in his own hands and he had no inclination to delegate work. His love of detail was perhaps his shortcoming, as it added enormously to his own work, which was often irritating to his subordinates. On the other hand, it may be that there were times when the government of such a sensitive organization as the Church was better off in the hands of one man alone. Who can say for certain? He was always thinking in terms of the Church's future centuries.

However, one must be extremely prudent in judging Pope Pius XII's thinking on international matters during World War II, since no personal diary or notes of his during that time have ever come to light. And it was only rarely that records were kept by the Vatican officials of conversations the Pope had with his intimate collaborators or even with important visitors from the outside, such as ministers, ambassadors, or private individuals offering information or suggestions. Sometimes, if the Cardinal Secretary of State or one of the undersecretaries happened to be present, reference would be made in their published documents to what the Holy Father had said, but only very briefly. It should always be remembered that, as Supreme Head of the Universal Church, his first concern was the welfare of Roman Catholics throughout the world irrespective of what their nationalities might be. The Secretariat of State, although generally looked upon as the foreign office of the Holy See, was unlike its counterparts in other countries in that, in its correspondence with Vatican diplomats abroad, its main concern was the religious life of the faithful rather than international politics. In fact, documents relating to the latter are surprisingly few.

There were absolutely no signs that the Pope was pro-Fascist or pro-Nazi. In fact, the opposite seemed more the case. Monsignor Tardini once told me that after Pope Pius XII's election to the papacy, he did not once meet Mussolini, and clearly had no desire to do so. However, seven years before his election in 1932, he had received a visit from Mussolini, who paid his respects to him as Secretary of State, after a formal visit to the then Pope Pius XI. That had been their only meeting and they never spoke again. Monsignor Tardini also recalled that *l'Osservatore Romano* was the only newspaper in the world which never used the familiar titles of "Il Duce" or "Chief of Fascism" when referring to Mussolini, but only the formal "Prime Minister of Italy," "The President of the Council of Ministers," or "The Chief of the Italian Government." Nor did *l'Osservatore Romano* ever mention Hitler as the "Fuehrer," but only as the "Chancellor of the Reich." This attitude of studied aloofness on the part of the Holy See was regarded as unfriendly, annoying both Mussolini and Hitler.

By describing the Pope as a charming man, I do not for one moment overlook his great spiritual qualities. Whether near him or away from him, one was always conscious of them. To me, he was definitely a spiritual man, though perhaps not saintly the way Pope Pius X had been. Pope Pius XII was often described as a political Pope, which he seemed to me to be at the time. Very possibly the future will rate him a saint. Only time will tell.

Friends living in Rome who occasionally came to lunch or tea with us had no way of communicating with us beforehand, so they would simply drop in informally, always, however, with a special written permit from the Vatican authorities who invariably notified the Italian police. Furthermore, even if they were priests, it was necessary for them to exhibit their permits to the Swiss Guards at the Vatican entrance, and later to the Vatican gendarmes at the gateway of Santa Marta.

Two American clerics, Monsignor William Hemmick and Father Joseph McGeough, brought us news of Rome from time to time. The former was a Canon at the Church of Santa Maria Maggiore and lived in an attractive apartment in the center of Rome. Although he was not really supposed to come and see us, Monsignor Hemmick would sneak in and greet us with some remark such as, "Well, I got by the guards that time!" Father McGeough lived at the American College situated on the Janiculum Hill near the Vatican. His work was mainly with the Congregation of the Oriental Church, but he was also connected with the Secretariat of State, so access to our quarters was less of a problem for him than for the others.

One of our favorites among the clergy was a lively Irishman, Monsignor Hugh O'Flaherty of the Supreme Sacred Congregation of the Holy Office. His activities in finding safe hiding places, both inside the Vatican and elsewhere, for Allied escaped prisoners of war and for other refugees from the Germans, made him literally famous. He lived practically next door to us, just outside the Vatican walls, on the Via Teutonica; he often came into Santa Marta on business and delighted us with his countless amusing stories. An excellent golfer, he gave golf lessons in the Vatican gardens to the Chinese Minister, but the golf balls eventually disappeared without a trace into the numerous fountains in the gardens.

Inside the walls, our closest friend among the clerics was the Belgian Jesuit Father Emmanuel Mistiaen, the French speaker on the Vatican radio. He lived in the radio building at the top of the hill in the Vatican Gardens. During the nine-month German occupation of Rome, while our two boys stayed with us, Pére Mistiaen arranged to have the Jesuit fathers of the radio give them lessons. On his initiative, the boys also broadcast over the radio, under assumed names of course, a children's program which was heard in the United States and in Europe.

Our other social contacts inside the walls involved mainly

our diplomatic colleagues and their families. By September 1942, there were thirteen chiefs-of-mission, eight of them from Latin America, residing inside the Vatican. In early 1943, the Nationalist Chinese Minister joined the group. Members of the Vatican Secretariat of State with whom I did business were frequently invited by us for lunch or tea, but they rarely accepted. I could never persuade even the American representative in the Secretariat of State, Father Walter Carroll, to accept our hospitality. Because of the desire of the Holy See to protect its neutral position at all costs, the personnel of the Secretariat were not supposed to maintain other than strictly official contacts with the Allied diplomats.

Among our diplomatic colleagues in Santa Marta, the British Minister, D'Arcy Osborne, was our closest friend; we saw him nearly every day. If we did not lunch or dine together, he would come to us for coffee and a cognac in the evening before returning to the BBC 10:45 P.M. news, which he faithfully monitored every night for the Holy Father. Tall and lean, he combined an unusual grace, elegance, and dignity. He was a great reader and a talented watercolor artist, and although a bachelor, he was fond of children and was much loved by our boys. He had been accredited to the Holy See since 1936, moving into the Vatican City in 1940, and his acute and well-balanced judgment was often sought after. On summer afternoons he would enthusiastically join the tennis games on the Ethiopian College court.

The French Ambassador Leon Bérard, his wife, and adolescent daughter, who we called "La Petite Marguerite," lived on the floor below the British Legation. Monsieur Bérard, 66 years old, had been a distinguished member of the French Academy. Besides being an author, he had held many posts in the French Government and was very much an intellectual of the old school. From certain indications on his face, he was also partial

Pius XII addressing Romans from St. Peter's.

Harold
Tittmann, Jr.,
and
Myron Taylor
with Swiss
Guards.

D'Arcy Osborne.

Myron Taylor.

Tittmann family in Santa Marta apartment garden.

"Palazzino" or annex of Santa Marta, home of American and Yugoslav representatives to the Vatican.

Meeting of
Myron Taylor
and Pius XII.

First reception of Myron Taylor by Cardinal Maglione
on February 27, 1940.

Eleanor Tittmann, Harold H. Tittmann, Jr., and Myron Taylor
in Tittmann living room, 1942.

Harold H. Tittmann III, Vatican 1943 *(left)*.
Barclay Tittmann, Vatican 1943 *(right)*.

Harold H. Tittmann, Jr., after Papal audience, December 1943.

Escaped British POW refugees at the Vatican with Osborne's
assistant, Hugh Montgomery, and Barclay Tittmann, center.

German soldiers
retreating from Rome,
June 4, 1944.
Photographed by
Harold H. Tittmann III
from the walls
of the Vatican.

Harold H. Tittmann, Jr., at work on his memoirs,
Manchester, Massachusetts, 1978.

to the old-world habit of taking snuff. When appointed Ambassador in December 1940, he was obliged to reside in the Vatican City because the Franco-Italian Armistice of June 1940, while ending military activities, did not terminate the legal state of war between the two countries.

Bérard was a loyal representative of the Vichy Government and therefore his relations with his Allied colleagues were necessarily restricted. Although faithful to Marshal Pétain, he was not pro-Axis and never associated himself with Laval's policies. His closest advisor was the Reverend Father Martin Gillet, a picturesque Frenchman who was also believed to be loyal to Pétain. To suggestions from their friends in the Vatican that they might adopt a stiffer attitude toward the Germans, both Bérard and Gillet invariably answered, with a shrug of their shoulders, *Qu'est-ce que vous voulez, les Allemands sont les maîtres.* ("What can you do, the Germans are the masters.") In April 1942, Laval offered Bérard a cabinet position in the Vichy Government, but Bérard refused, explaining that he preferred his quiet post at the Vatican.

Of course, we never shared a meal with the Bérards, but now and then we would see them in the Gardens. Madame Bérard was clearly resentful of the Allies, as evidenced by her disapproving looks after Allied successes. She did, however, have a sense of humor. One hot afternoon when we were walking in the Gardens, our cocker spaniel suddenly disappeared and could not be found, though we could hear his whimpers. We were looking under and around every bush when suddenly "Madame Vichy" (as our boys called Madame Bérard) appeared and asked, *Qu'est-ce que vous faites ici, vous jouez à cache-cache?* ("What are you doing here—playing hide-and-seek?") It was the only time she had ever spoken to us. The French Embassy typist was also distant and unfriendly and we called her "La marche funèbre," as it always seemed as if she were participating in a funeral, walking as she did without a smile and never a glimmer of recognition.

In striking contrast, the French Counselor of Embassy, Jacques de Blesson, was pro-Ally and strongly opposed to the policies of Marshal Pétain. De Blesson was certain that Pétain was slowly, perhaps unwittingly, drifting into the hands of the Nazis. During the hot summer of 1942, when our courtyard windows were wide open, I could often hear Bérard and de Blesson arguing in loud angry tones over the Vichy situation, but de Blesson was unable to convince his chief of Pétain's incompetence. Finally, in November, the two French diplomats agreed to disagree and this brought their precarious relationship to an end at last.

We frequently saw the Polish Ambassador, Casimir Papée, and his wife, who lived on the floor between the de Blessons and the Bérards. It was, however, a source of despair to D'Arcy and ourselves that such gentle people should have two such vicious fox terriers. Papée, a small, dapper man, would rush through the Gardens with his dogs as if pulled by a pair of lions. They attacked everything, once causing D'Arcy to exclaim unhappily: "I fear they have just done in my favorite cat!" The dogs of Santa Marta were a prominent feature of our life, and they must have been of some concern to the Vatican. Each time a dog was taken for a walk, the exact time was marked in the guard's notebook posted at the entrance of Santa Marta, along with the posted arrivals and departures of the diplomats and their guests.

Kosta Zukic, the young Yugoslav representative, lived just below us with his wife Betsa. Despite their many anxieties, the Zukics, both Orthodox Serbs from Belgrade, maintained one of the most cheerful households and were known for their hospitality. They spoke Parisian French and throughout the war years Betsa somehow preserved a marvelous "chic." Kosta, well-groomed with black hair and a flowery mustache, was very much a Serb, prideful and touchy on the subject of his country. I was struck by how seriously the Zukics took the war. For the Yugoslavs, especially the Serbs, the Nazi victories had been complete disasters. Until the arrival of the Chinese Minister, who was a Buddhist, the only non-Catholics within the Vatican City were the Zukics, D'Arcy and his household, and our family with my secretary.

In March 1942, the Italian Government ordered Latin American diplomats accredited to the Holy See from Brazil, Bolivia, Colombia, Cuba, Ecuador, Peru, Venezuela, and Uruguay, whose countries had declared war on Italy, to leave Rome for the Vatican City, but it was not until late summer that suitable quarters could be arranged for them. Santa Marta being completely filled, this additional influx of diplomatic guests was lodged in the Palazzo del Tribunale, a four-storied building situated in the back of St. Peter's at the entrance of the Vatican Gardens. Once more the Vatican displaced a considerable number of its own citizens, made expensive alterations including the installation of a passenger elevator, and transformed the building into a series of comfortable apartments.

The Latin Americans were a welcome addition to our diplomatic community and brightened our lives with cheerful little champagne parties, not having the same financial restrictions which had been imposed on us. The Brazilian ambassador, Dr. Ildebrando Pompeo Accioly, was the dean of the diplomatic corps inside the Vatican. A well-known international lawyer, he was a pillar of strength to his colleagues and courageous in his support of the Allied cause.

During the following winter, in February 1943, the Chinese Minister, Dr. Cheou Kang Sie and his Secretary, Dr. R. H. Ouang, were accredited to the Vatican where they joined the Latin Americans living in the Palazzo del Tribunale, thus completing our circle totaling fourteen chiefs-of-mission living within the Vatican walls. Dr. Sie was a scholar with numerous published works to his credit, including an account of the early life of Marshal Chiang Kai-shek, yet he entered into our attempts at more light-hearted diversions with touching enthusiasm, introducing the game of golf in the Vatican Gardens.

The first major issue (in reality, a "tempest in a teapot") that my father had to confront after his move into the Vatican was the request of the Japanese Government to establish formal diplomatic relations with the Holy See:

On February 4, with Allied military and naval fortunes seemingly at their nadir, I was asked to call on the Cardinal Secretary of State, who told me that the Japanese Government intended to establish a diplomatic mission to the Holy See. Maglione said that the Holy See would not be in a position to refuse, because of the widespread interests of the Catholic Church in Japan and Japanese-occupied territories. He added that he was informing beforehand the U.S. and British representatives as a matter of courtesy, hoping that the news would be held in the strictest confidence by their governments pending a public announcement. Maglione explained that the Japanese had considered such a move several times in the past, but had not followed through because of internal opposition from the Buddhists.

In hearing what the Cardinal had to say, I could not help making a "wry face." I told him that the acceptance by the Holy See of a Japanese diplomatic mission at this time would not go down well in the United States. Maglione replied that naturally he could understand our reaction, but repeated that the Holy

See had no choice but to accept. I pointed out that this was obviously a war-related move by Japan, and I wondered whether by
the same token the Holy See would be willing to accredit representatives from other belligerent countries, as, for example,
Soviet Russia. The Cardinal laughed and remarked: "At any
rate those gentlemen have not asked so far." I gathered from the
attitude of the Cardinal that the Vatican might welcome an
approach by the Soviets to establish diplomatic relations, and
Mgr. Montini later told me that he personally thought such a
move might be acceptable, especially if Stalin could thereby be
persuaded to adopt a more moderate attitude towards religion.

Following my meeting with Maglione, I called on Mgrs.
Montini and Tardini, who admitted that the news of the Japanese initiative had descended upon them like a bolt of lightning.
They pointed out, however, that (1) in Tokyo there had been an
Apostolic Delegate representing the Vatican for the past twenty-
five years and an Archbishop for fifty years; (2) a number of bish-
oprics were now established in various parts of Japan; and (3)
increasing numbers of Catholics were falling each day under the
domination of the Japanese as their armies advanced. Therefore,
diplomatic relations between Japan and the Holy See could
prove beneficial to the extensive interests of the Church in the
Far East. Tardini said that while he recognized that the Japanese
motivation was undoubtedly to influence Catholic opinion in
their favor, the establishment of a Japanese mission to the Vatican would provide the Holy See with additional means to exert a
moderating influence on the Japanese authorities.

My own reactions on the spot appeared mild compared to
the furor engendered at the White House and the Department
of State by the news of the acceptance by the Vatican of a Japanese mission, despite my having expressed the following thoughts
in a telegram to Washington:

It is difficult to see how the Holy See could have refused the Japanese request. By virtue of its acknowledged universality and its mission of peace and goodwill toward all alike, the door cannot very well be closed to any particular state seeking to establish diplomatic relations with it.

Not so in the eyes of Washington, however. When Mgr. Vagnozzi of the Apostolic Delegation in Washington explained the Vatican's position, Under Secretary of State Sumner Welles told him that he considered the Holy See's decision "deplorable" and "incredible," since at the very moment unspeakable atrocities were being committed by the Japanese in areas under their control, Catholic communities and churches in the Philippines were being violated and desecrated, and the announced policy of the Japanese military leaders was to eliminate the influence of the white race, including Christianity, in the Far East. In conclusion, Welles expressed the hope that the Vatican's decision be reconsidered.

According to Welles, Mgr. Vagnozzi seemed to agree with him entirely, realizing that the Holy See's action would have disastrous effects on public opinion in the United States. A few days later, the Apostolic Delegate himself called on Welles and confided to him that he had already informed the Vatican of his full agreement with the U.S. point of view. According to Welles, Cicognani "seemed profoundly disturbed and utterly unable to comprehend any justifiable reason for [the Vatican's decision.]." Welles informed him that President Roosevelt "found the report completely impossible to credit," since he knew the Holy Father and his views personally. The President believed "that the American public would interpret the event as an important victory for Japan."

Towards the end of February, the news of the Japanese initiative and the American protests was leaked to the press, allegedly by the Foreign Office in London. The news surprised the Germans, and may have inspired them to fabricate and publish through the official Italian news agency the text of a personal letter from Stalin to the Pope which stated that if Japan could have an ambassador to the Holy See, Moscow should have the right to be represented there also. The Germans apparently hoped that the letter, even though obviously fictitious, might draw an anti-Soviet public statement from the Holy See which they could use in support of their campaign against Russia. But the Vatican's only reaction was to protest to the Italian authorities the publication of the phony letter.

The "leak" worked against the interests of the United States and Great Britain, since it made it impossible for the Holy See to reconsider its decision to receive a Japanese mission, which would have been viewed as an un-neutral submission to Allied pressure. Cardinal Maglione, after the publication of the Stalin letter, seemed to have "gone cold" on the idea of diplomatic relations with the Soviets. When I saw him on March 16, he emphasized to me that a Soviet representative would only be acceptable to the Holy See if it were satisfied that the Soviets had completely changed their policy towards religious matters. We also discussed the "leak," which greatly upset the Cardinal. He seemed convinced that the British were determined to scotch the Japanese initiative by any means in their power. The British believed that this was yet another instance of the Holy See yielding to Axis pressure. However, Japan had played a lone hand, working mostly through the Apostolic Delegation in Tokyo, without German or Italian involvement. Later, the Foreign Office denied in a message to Maglione that it was responsible for the "leak."

During our meeting, I presented to Maglione, as instructed by Washington, a written statement of the views of Sumner

Welles. The Cardinal said that he had already received much the same information from the Apostolic Delegation in Washington; he told me quite frankly that he was unable to understand the lack of comprehension on our part of the Holy See's position. He stated that the Vatican did not have sufficient elements of proof of the alleged wartime atrocities attributed to the Japanese by the Americans to enable him to pass judgment thereon or allow them to influence the Holy See in the formulation of policy. The Cardinal then rather cuttingly added that the question raised by Mr. Welles as to whether the Holy See's efforts to protect the purely spiritual interests of Catholics under Japanese domination were worthwhile or not, might well have been left to the judgment of the Holy See which had long experience in things spiritual. Maglione concluded by mentioning that he had heard nothing further from the Japanese concerning their intentions and that speaking personally he earnestly hoped that he would not.

In an effort to defuse the controversy, the Pope had addressed a personal message to President Roosevelt explaining the reasons for the Vatican's decision. He pointed out that the Vatican could not refuse a request by a foreign power to enter into diplomatic relations; that the Holy See had major interests in Japan and the Far East; that the Holy See's impartial outlook on the war was greatly strengthened by the presence near the Pope of representatives from the belligerents; and that the establishment of diplomatic relations with Japan did not imply approval of all the activities of that country. The Pope appealed to the President to prevent the entirely justifiable position of the Holy See from being misinterpreted.

On March 26, Japan formally requested approval for its representative to the Holy See, Mr. Ken Harada, who had been Japanese chargé d'affaires at Vichy; this was accorded by the

Vatican two days later. At a press conference on April 5, President Roosevelt admitted that he had been persuaded by the validity of the Holy See's arguments and asked the newsmen to forget about the uproar surrounding the issue. He said that he now realized that the Holy See could not have done otherwise in view of its interests in the Far East. Apparently Archbishop Spellman of New York was instrumental in changing the President's attitude. Spellman believed that contacts through the Church in Japanese-controlled areas could be useful to the Allies, particularly with respect to prisoners of war in Japanese hands. Harada presented his letters of credence to the Pope on May 9, as Special Delegate of Japan to the Holy See with the rank of ambassador. Thus ended this brief but acrimonious dispute between the Vatican and the United States.

Since our two countries were at war, I did not communicate personally with Ambassador Harada, and it was unlikely that we would even meet casually since Harada and his staff were based in Rome. I nevertheless heard from various sources that he was a fine gentleman and an excellent diplomat. On a few occasions, such as the Pope's Christmas midnight mass, where all accredited diplomats were present, we saw each other at a distance. However, we did have one unexpected close confrontation during one of my visits to Mgr. Montini's office on the top floor of the Vatican Palace. As I approached the elevator I saw that the operator was beckoning me to hurry in as apparently he could wait no longer. Inside the elevator I found myself literally rubbing shoulders with Harada along with the newly appointed German Ambassador, Baron Ernst von Weizsacker, my two principal enemy colleagues. As the narrow, old-fashioned elevator proceeded upwards slowly to its destination, all we could do at first in this embarrassing situation was to try to ignore each other by looking the other way. However, upon arrival at the top floor, when the operator motioned to us that we could leave the elevator, a decision had to be made as to which of the three diplomats should have the honor of being the first to get out. With considerable relief, we started to look at each other and exchanged smiles. After much bowing and scraping by all three of us, the two ambassadors decided that I should be the lucky one. So contrary to established protocol, out went the chargé d'affaires of the United States ahead of the ambassadors of his country's worst enemies, Japan and Germany.

Although the United States Government had failed to prevent the appointment of a Japanese ambassador to the Holy See, it now sought to counterbalance the situation by seeking the prompt establishment of diplomatic relations between the Vatican and additional Allied governments, especially the Nationalist Chinese Government in Chungking. I was instructed to request an audience with the Holy Father for this purpose, and was received by the Pope on April 2. When I emphasized to him the continued unhappiness in Washington concerning the Japanese mission to the Holy See, the Pope told me that he realized that, coming so soon after Pearl Harbor, this had caused bitter feelings in the United States. But since the Vatican had nothing whatever to do with the timing, it should not be blamed for this. I then informed the Pope that we were hoping that relations between the Holy See and the governments of Nationalist China and the Netherlands could be inaugurated "immediately." The Holy Father noted that the establishment of a Chinese mission was already under discussion and had his approval, but doubted that representation at the Vatican of the Netherlands Government-in-exile based in London was necessary at this time.

The Vatican agreed on June 16 to accept Cheou Kang Sie, a diplomat attached to the Chinese Nationalist Legation in Bern, as the Chinese Minister to the Holy See. Sie did not take up residence in the Vatican City until the beginning of 1943, because the Vatican had difficulties in finding adequate quarters for the Chinese mission. The Vatican's decision upset the Japanese Government, which regarded it as an un-neutral act in view of the existence of a second Chinese government sponsored by Japan in Nanking. Harada proposed that the Vatican should also receive a representative from that government, but Cardinal Maglione refused. The Vatican eventually agreed to send a Delegate to deal with Catholic interests in areas of China occupied by Japan.

In spite of its disapproval of the acceptance by the Vatican of a Japanese mission, the British Government urgently solicited the assistance of the Holy See in June 1942 to obtain information regarding the welfare of British prisoners in Japanese hands. In 1943, the Vatican informed the State Department that its representative in Tokyo had visited on several occasions American and British prisoner-of-war camps in Japan, distributing food and books. Thus American and British prisoners may have ultimately benefited from the formal ties between Japan and the Vatican.

The establishment of diplomatic relations by the Holy See and Finland in July 1942, for the first time in history, may have been related to Allied reactions to the Japanese issue. Finland was now an ally of Germany and had joined the war against the Soviet Union. Although both the Finns and the Vatican denied that the move had anything to do with Nazi pressure on the Finns, the Allies had just finished asking for the establishment of missions from two of their governments, China and the Netherlands, to counterbalance the new Japanese embassy. In view of the timing, it seemed as though the Axis might have decided to even up the score through the Finns. The new

Finnish Minister, George Achates Gripenberg, paid an official call on me on August 24. While Great Britain had declared war on Finland at the insistence of the Soviet Union, the United States had not followed suit. Gripenberg emphasized that his presence at the Vatican was purely a Finnish move, with no German influence. He said that one of the primary reasons for the move was to demonstrate appreciation for the traditional friendship between Finland and the Holy See, and especially for the warmth with which Pius XII personally supported Finland when it was attacked by Russia in the "Winter War." The arrival of the Finnish Minister meant that there were now 42 countries represented at the Vatican, making it all the more important, it seemed to me, that the United States have a representative present, especially since this "listening post" now included two Asian diplomatic missions.

During the controversy over the establishment of a Japanese embassy, the Holy See had adopted a cautious and perhaps skeptical attitude when confronted by American allegations of "unspeakable" atrocities committed by the Japanese. The Vatican reacted similarly in dealing with Allied demands that it condemn Nazi atrocities in Europe, a subject that occupied my father throughout 1942:

Because of German invasions of various European countries, Pope Pius XII found himself faced by a dilemma: Should he should speak openly against these aggressions or remain silent? It was the subject of much discussion, some very bitter, by the Allies and sometimes by the Axis. For instance, it was difficult to understand why the Holy Father maintained a prudent reserve during several days after the invasion of Poland, a very Catholic country, when he did not hesitate one second to publicly express his sympathy the following spring for victims of the

Nazi attacks on the Netherlands (which had a large non-Catholic community), Belgium, and Luxembourg.

There were several explanations for the Pope's silence with regard to Poland. The Pope was aware, even during the first few days after the Nazi invasion began, that Mussolini was busy contacting Hitler and the governments of England, France, and Poland in an effort to bring about another "Munich Conference." The Holy Father viewed this particular plan with suspicion as it seemed a compromise solution which could easily have put the neo-pagan Nazis into a dominant position, greatly impairing the Church's influence. Therefore, he refrained from lending Vatican support to Mussolini's project. On the other hand, the Pope felt that, with the peace of the world at stake, he should take no steps, such as denouncing the Nazi aggressions, which might interfere with any progress toward ending the war, even though the peace arrived at might not be exactly to his liking.

There was something else which caused the Pope to be hesitant. He had been receiving reports during the month of August 1939 and even before from the Apostolic Nuncio in Warsaw, Monsignor Filippo Cortesi, indicating that a rigid attitude had been assumed by the Polish Foreign Minister, Colonel Josef Beck, and his entourage, in negotiations with the Germans. The Vatican, therefore, was not completely convinced at the outset of the Nazi invasion that it was the Germans alone who were responsible for the failure to find an agreement. Finally, there was always the threat of Nazi retaliation against Roman Catholic populations, should the Pope speak out.

In October 1939, the Jesuit-operated Vatican Radio started to broadcast first-hand accounts of atrocities perpetrated by the Nazis in Poland as reported to the Holy See by its own informants in that country. However, the Polish bishops hastened to notify the Vatican that after each broadcast had come over the air, the various local populations suffered "terrible" reprisals. The thought that there were those paying with their lives for the information publicized by the Vatican Radio made the continuation of these broadcasts impossible. The Superior General of the Jesuits, Father Ledochowski, personally gave the order to desist. He later told the French speaker on the Radio's staff: "How I hated to give the order to stop these broadcasts, especially since I am a Pole myself. But what else could one do? They [the Nazis] have the power and they use it as they please."

Nazi atrocities as well as Communist ones perpetrated against the overwhelmingly Catholic Polish people were first brought formally to the attention of the Vatican in a series of memoranda during the months of September and October in 1940 by the Polish Ambassador to the Holy See, Casimir Papée. The acts cited were: Soviet deportations of one and a half million Poles to the steppes of Central Asia; confiscation of property by the Nazis in a single province, Poznania, depriving 3600 families of their patrimony; the barbarous and infamous procedure of the sterilization of the young; forced labor inflicted on hundreds of thousands of persons, many of whom were incapable of manual labor and who were literally dragged from their homes; and finally the sending of one million Polish workers to Germany.

According to Papée's memorandum dated October 29, 1940, a copy of which was forwarded to Myron Taylor in the United States, the Polish people did not understand why they could not hear directly from the lips of the Holy Father himself his words of consolation and moral support in their fight for justice. Why did he not disapprove openly of the misdeeds of their enemies "who were also enemies of Christ"? The Vatican Radio, the memorandum continued, had been referring from time to time to atrocities committed in that part of Poland occupied by the Soviets, but nothing or almost nothing had been heard recently as to what the Nazis themselves had been doing. In fact, Ambassador Papée said *l'Osservatore Romano* had seemingly been maintaining silence on the entire question to the extent that even the word "Poland" had disappeared from its columns for months at a time, giving the impression that the unfortunate country was doomed to oblivion insofar as the Vatican was concerned.

According to Papée's memorandum, the Vatican thesis that there was no point in exasperating the oppressors by revealing their guilt was rejected by the greater part of the Polish people, who were convinced that the Germans above all feared public exposure of their crimes and understood only the strongest language. Papée pointed out that, when in January 1940 the Vatican Radio did happen to speak out in a series of broadcasts which stigmatized the Nazi occupation regime, the name of Germany was covered with shame. The resultant powerful reaction of world opinion had caused German authorities to hesitate in their criminal course and the entire population of Poland was able to benefit from the pause. However, the German Government, feeling the need to dispel the hurtful image created, successfully arranged, in March 1940, an audience with the Holy Father for Foreign Minister von Ribbentrop. According to Papée, the mere fact that the Supreme Pontiff had agreed to receive such an important Nazi official enabled the Nazi propagandists to claim that the Vatican approved of German policies. As a result, the Polish people felt that there was no point in continuing their resistance while hoping for the support of the Holy See.

In October 1941, numerous reports of wartime atrocities were beginning to reach the Vatican. I informed the State Department on October 27 that, although I had heard nothing

but praise in the Vatican for the forthright condemnation of the
Nazis two days earlier by President Roosevelt for their execution of hostages in Nantes, France, it did not appear that the
Holy Father was prepared to make any public protest on the
subject. The reason given was the usual one, namely that if
the Pope should openly reprove Nazi actions, the Nazis in return
would only vent their displeasure by bringing upon the Catholic
population even greater suffering. I added that, according to
Monsignor Montini, the Nuncio in Berlin had received urgent
instructions to intervene with the German Government on
behalf of the unfortunate victims, but that this démarche on the
part of the Holy Father was not generally known. In the opinion of the Polish Ambassador, greater publicity should have
been given by the Allies to the execution of hostages in Poland
by the Nazis, since the numbers involved were much larger
than in France. I could not help but sympathize with Papée's
views and reported them to the State Department in a letter
dated November 18, 1941.

Six months later, on May 22, 1942, the Polish Ambassador
spoke to the Cardinal Secretary of State about the wave of terror
organized by the Nazis in Poland at that moment and asked
whether there was not something the Holy See could do about
it. Maglione replied that frequently the Vatican was unable to
produce proof in light of German denials and explained that
Vatican intervention was not always opportune and occasionally had in fact the opposite effect to the one desired. Papée argued
that since the Nazi atrocities were so notorious, it was obvious
that no proof was needed. The Polish people, he said, desired
not so much the Vatican's intervention in individual cases but a
general condemnation of the methods employed by the Germans. The Ambassador added that the Poles believed that the
Nazi terror was bound to continue no matter what happened,

so that the population as a whole could not be any worse off in the future than it was now even if the Holy Father were to speak out.

In defense of his own position, the Pope, during one of his meetings in September 1942 with Myron Taylor, objected to the Polish Government-in-exile's eagerness to have him denounce the Nazis in public without sufficiently understanding the delicate position of the Holy See. The Pope pointed out that, while criticizing him for his silence, the Poles were the first to acknowledge their gratefulness for the paternal concern he had shown them in private messages and acts of charity. He had, furthermore, sent confidential communications to the Archbishop of Cracow, Adamo Stefano Sapieha, to the Cardinal Primate of Poland, Augusto Cardinal Hlond, and to the Prime Minister of the Polish Government-in-exile in London, General Ladislas Sikorski, all of the messages bearing words of sympathy for the unfortunate predicament of the Polish people. The Holy Father emphasized to Mr. Taylor that he never overlooked an opportunity to protest Nazi misdeeds to the German authorities through regular diplomatic channels in Berlin.

The position taken by the Polish Ambassador Papée in 1940 and afterwards, urging the Pope to speak out, appeared to be in conflict with that of the Polish bishops in 1939 when they appealed to Father General Ledochowski to have the Vatican Radio cease its references to Nazi atrocities in Poland. This difference apparently arose because the Ambassador was taking his instructions from the Polish Government-in-exile in London and had no direct communication with the bishops on the spot in Poland.

On June 16, 1942, I reported to the Department of State that a stream of criticism of the Pope was emanating from pro-Allied sources in the Vatican because of his persistent refusal to speak out against the violation of moral and natural laws by the Nazis. The Holy Father seemed to occupy himself with spiritual matters, charitable acts, and rhetoric while adopting at the same time an ostrichlike policy toward atrocities that were obvious to everyone. I myself asked Cardinal Maglione whether the Holy See could not take some action regarding massacres of hostages that were then taking place in Bohemia and Moravia, and pointed out that some success had already been achieved by the Pope's representatives with local German authorities in France on behalf of hostages in that country. Maglione replied that the two situations were not comparable, because Bohemia and Moravia constituted a protectorate of Germany, in other words an integral part of the Reich regarding which the Nazis could be expected to brook no interference from any quarter, while France, on the other hand, although partially occupied, continued to maintain its sovereignty as an independent country.

Two opposite interpretations of the Pope's position were prevalent inside the Vatican City. One was that the chief reason for the silence of the Pope was his conviction even at this late hour that the Axis was bound to win the war and that he did not wish, therefore, to jeopardize the future position of the Holy See by speaking out now against the future victors. But there were also those who believed that, while the Holy Father was still impressed by the military might of Germany and Japan, his policy was in reality founded on the assumption that the Allies were ultimately destined to win the war. If that were to happen, the status of the Church in Germany and the freedom of the faithful would be fully restored and in the meantime there would be no point in subjecting the Catholic population in that country to additional hardships while the war was in progress through anti-Nazi denunciations. They also believed that the Pope regarded the Allies and not the Nazis as friends of the

Church and that because they were his friends he could risk their temporary displeasure by not speaking out, knowing that eventually all would be understood. They were certain that if the Pope ever became convinced that the Nazis were going to be the victors and thus gain a free hand in Europe, he would lose no time in attacking them with every spiritual and moral weapon at his disposal and, if necessary, lead the Church to martyrdom. If in time the Nazis were to force the Pope to leave Rome, the moral influence of the Papacy would be immeasurably increased by just such an event.

Another reason given for the Pope's silence was that he was always hoping for the opportune moment to play the part of mediator between the belligerent powers. In the meantime, he had to be careful not to compromise his chances by public utterances which could raise the question of his complete impartiality. There had been occasions when the Axis had also called upon him to break his silence. For instance, Hitler had demanded the Holy See's approval of the Nazi "crusade" against Russia and also the Pope's public condemnation of the Allied bombings of German cities such as Cologne. The Pope complied with neither demand.

Accioly, the Brazilian ambassador, came to see me on July 29, 1942, to ask me whether I was prepared to join him and other colleagues inside the Vatican in separate but simultaneous approaches to the Holy Father to persuade him to condemn publicly the Nazi atrocities perpetrated in German-occupied areas. I submitted the question to the Department of State and immediately received a favorable reply. Informing Accioly of our agreement, I told him I planned to leave a memorandum with the Cardinal Secretary of State pointing out the helpful effect a condemnation by the Holy Father would have in restraining the barbarous actions of the Nazis.

At the same time Accioly, together with my British and Uruguayan colleagues, took similar steps, followed a few days later by the Peruvian and Cuban envoys. The Belgian, Polish, and Yugoslav representatives, whose countries were occupied by the Nazis, had already made a joint démarche of their own on September 12 on the same subject, but unrelated to the Accioly proposal. Although we learned that the Holy Father was giving careful consideration to the notes, Vatican officials believed that there were too many countries involved to keep the matter confidential, so that if the Pope had spoken out then he would have laid himself open to the accusation of having yielded to Allied pressure. This did not mean that the Pope was not reserving the right to call injustice and violence by their proper names, if not publicly to the world, certainly in the communications from the Holy See to individual governments. Furthermore, the Holy See was still convinced that any forthright denunciations by the Pope, at least insofar as Poland was concerned, would have resulted in the deaths of many more people, and on this point claimed to be better informed with regard to this danger than the various Allied governments-in-exile who constantly kept pressing the Holy Father. In any event, the Vatican took no public action on the Accioly-initiated representations.

I prepared a summary in September 1942 of the principal arguments used in Vatican circles in support of the Pope's silence with respect to the condemnation of Nazi atrocities:

1. There is constant pressure on the Holy See from the Axis powers to denounce alleged Allied atrocities and, because of its own silence, the Holy See is often accused of being pro-Ally. The Holy See could not very well condemn, for instance, certain Nazi atrocities without saying something about Russian cruelties as well. Granted that many of these alleged Allied atrocities are insignificant when

compared to those perpetrated by the Nazis, it would not be an easy matter for the Pope to distinguish degrees of violation of moral and natural laws and he would need cognizance of all reputed violations, however great or small, in the process. While the war was going on, it was virtually impossible for any belligerent to obtain proof of alleged atrocities. Of course, such atrocities were also used by both sides as propaganda.

2. Should the Pope embark upon a policy of denunciation of all the moral and natural laws violated in wartime, wherever and by whomever committed, the Holy See would be obliged to spend a great deal of time, first in investigation and then in denunciation. It would, in fact, have tended to develop into an organization whose major activity might well become the determination of the facts and the adjudging of the guilty. The difficulties in assembling supporting evidence of reported violations in order to justify condemnatory action would be enormous.

3. The public pronouncements by the Pope on the moral law must stand the test of time. The danger of error involved in descending to the particular amidst the heat of war passions was obvious.

4. The Pope, on a number of occasions, had already openly condemned major offenses against morality in wartime. The terms have been general but the world well knew to whom the words of condemnation were addressed.

5. When members of the hierarchy speak out on violations, as they have done in Germany and other countries, it should be realized that it is the voice of the Pope speaking and that this should be sufficient. It is common knowledge that when bishops make public statements on important subjects, they do so with the prior approval of

their superior, the Supreme Pontiff. Numerous bishops in occupied Europe spoke out against the Germans, and many were put in jail.

6. The Holy See is firmly convinced that any public statement by the Pope condemning Nazi atrocities in Nazi-occupied Europe, far from doing any good, would greatly worsen the already precarious situation of Catholics obliged to reside in those areas. No lives would be saved thereby. On the contrary, many more would be lost. The Vatican claims to be better informed on this phase of the matter than the governments-in-exile who keep urging the Holy Father to speak out.

As I recall, the question of extermination, rather than persecution which we all knew about, of the Jews in Poland by the Nazis did not come to the attention of the diplomats in the Vatican City until the fall of 1942. On September 26, Mr. Taylor forwarded to Cardinal Maglione information regarding the liquidation of the Warsaw ghetto and massacres of Jews by the Germans contained in a letter dated August 30 from the Geneva office of the Jewish Agency for Palestine. The letter alleged that corpses of Jews were used for making fats, and their bones for the manufacture of fertilizer. In a third-person note, unsigned, Maglione replied on October 10 that unverified reports of severe measures taken against non-Aryans had also reached the Holy See from other sources. However, the Cardinal assured Taylor that the Holy See was taking every opportunity in order to mitigate the sufferings of non-Aryans.

With regard to the Fascist Government's attitude toward the Jews, a decree was issued in March 1939 ordering foreign Jews to leave Italy, but nobody paid much attention; the foreign Jewish population in the country actually increased from 2000 to over 7000 by November of that year. After Italy had declared war on France and England in June 1940, foreign Jews were interned in 30 concentration camps, or confined to 400 special areas called "confinos."

In June 1942, the Rome newspaper *Il Messagero* published a photograph on the front page showing some fifty Jews at forced labor, digging ditches along the banks of the Tiber. The workers looked dejected and pathetic. This brutal and degrading act reported by one of the government-controlled Italian newspapers was so shocking to me that I wrote a personal letter on June 10 to Monsignor Montini, basing my protest on Article 1, Par. 2 of the Concordat between Italy and the Holy See which reads: "In consideration of the sacred character of the Eternal City, Episcopal See of the Supreme Pontiff, center of the Catholic world, and goal of pilgrimages, the Italian Government will take care to prevent in Rome everything that may be in contrast to the aforesaid character." I also brought the subject to the attention of the Cardinal Secretary of State, who had already seen my letter to Monsignor Montini. Cardinal Maglione said the photograph had aroused the indignation not only of the Vatican, but of all good Italians as well, and that he had therefore made an oral protest to the Italian Ambassador to the Holy See. Maglione did not, however, feel that the Holy See was in a position to make a public demonstration of its disapproval, as I had suggested. It was also clear to me that even if the Vatican organ, *l'Osservatore Romano,* should dare to speak out, its remonstrance would have been mild since the newspaper had only recently been under attack by the Axis for refusing to condemn a British air raid that had just taken place on the cathedral city of Cologne in Germany.

What the Pope was surely aware of, although not admitted in the Vatican at the time, was the danger that any specific statement by him in public against the Nazis would have been seized upon by Allied propaganda chiefs and exploited by them as an important weapon in winning the war. Nazi propagandists would have done the same thing if the Pope had spoken out against the Allies. Many of us who were eager to hear the Pope speak out realized that he could not do so without giving the impression that he was taking sides in the conflict. In my opinion the Holy Father should have declared to the world at the beginning of the hostilities that he intended to denounce all atrocities without exception, but that such denunciation would neither signify that he was taking sides nor affect in any way his traditional position "outside and above world political conflicts." With such a public declaration to fall back on, the Holy Father might have shown more resolve.

Another motive behind the Pope's disinclination to publicly denounce Nazi atrocities was his fear that if he should do so and Germany lose the war, the German people, in the bitterness of their defeat, would reproach him later for having contributed, if only morally and indirectly, to this defeat. Just such an accusation was directed against the Holy See by Germans after the First World War as the result of certain phrases spoken and because of attitudes adopted by Pope Benedict XV while hostilities were still in progress before the German defeat in 1918. Bearing in mind that Pius XII had thirteen years of conditioning in Germany as the representative of the Holy See, it was not surprising that, knowing the Germans well as he did, he sought to avoid the repetition of the unfortunate experience of one of his predecessors.

But Pope Pius XII never did speak out while the war was in progress, so there is no evidence from which to judge whether it was the right thing to do or not. If he had spoken out, would there have been fewer victims or more? There can be no final answer. Personally, I cannot help but feel that the Holy Father chose the better path by not speaking out and thereby saved many lives. Who can say what the Nazis would have done in their ruthless furor had they been further inflamed by public denunciations coming from the Holy See? It should also be remembered that the Nazi authorities were gradually realizing that they were destined to lose the war and the psychological effect of such blighted hopes could easily have caused them to react even more violently to outside pressure. To the wealth of information in the archives on similar situations garnered by the Vatican over the centuries, and to the help of expert historians using these archives, Pope Pius XII was able to add his unusual personal knowledge of the Nazi and German character. There was much inside information available to the Pontiff from secret sources. Who could have been more qualified than this Pope to decide under the circumstances?

In fact, the intense pressure from Allied diplomats may have induced the Pope, in his 1942 Christmas message, to make an apparent indirect reference to the alleged extermination of Jews by the Nazis. The Pope referred to "the hundreds of thousands who, through no fault of their own, and solely because of their nation or race, have been condemned to death or progressive wasting away." Pius XII received my father on December 30, 1942, who reported as follows to the State Department:

With regard to his Christmas message the Pope gave me the impression that he was sincere in believing that he had spoken therein clearly enough to satisfy all those who had been insisting in the past that he utter some word of condemnation of the Nazi atrocities and he seemed surprised when I told him that I thought there were some who did not share his belief. He said that he thought that it was plain to everyone that he was refer-ring to the Poles, Jews and hostages when he declared that hundreds of thousands of persons had been killed or tortured through no fault of their own, sometimes only because of their race or nationality. He explained that when talking of atrocities he could not name the Nazis without at the same time mentioning the Bolsheviks and this he thought might not be wholly pleasing to the Allies. He stated that he "feared" there was foundation for the atrocity reports of the Allies but led me to believe that he felt there had been some exaggeration for purpose of propaganda. Taken as a whole he thought his message should be welcomed by the American people and I agreed with him.

In a speech he gave at St. Louis University in 1961, my father recalled what the Pope had said on the subject of Nazi atrocities:

"One of the jobs Allied diplomats including myself undertook during the war was to persuade the Pope to come out in the open and denounce Hitler and the Nazis by name. We thought the Holy Father would eventually comply with our request because we knew that he detested the Nazi ideology and everything it stood for. But he never did. We had been keeping after him for quite a while and one day he said to us, a little impatiently: 'But why do you want me to point the finger and name names? I have already stated in three consecutive Christmas broadcasts that antireligious, totalitarian principles are iniquitous. These are the principles of the Nazis as any child can see.' We replied: 'But your broadcasts are too vague; they are open to many interpretations. We need something more explicit.' The Pope then explained: 'Well, I am sorry, I cannot do it and here are the reasons: first, there are over forty million German-speaking Catholics. If I should denounce the Nazis by name as you desire and Germany should lose the war, Germans everywhere would feel that I had contributed to the defeat, not only of

the Nazis, but of Germany herself; for the German population not to be able to make the distinction between the
Nazis and the Fatherland would only be human in the
confusion and distress of defeat. I cannot afford to risk
alienating so many of the faithful. One of my predecessors,
Pope Benedict XV in the First World War, through an
unfortunate public statement of the type you now wish me
to make, did just this and the interests of the Church in
Germany suffered as a result. Second, if I denounce the
Nazis by name I must in all justice do the same as regards
the Bolsheviks whose principles are strikingly similar; you
would not wish me to say such things about an ally of
yours at whose side you are engaged today in a death
struggle.' It was difficult for us to argue these points effectively with the Pope and in the end we were obliged to
resign ourselves to the failure of our attempts."

*President Roosevelt's desire to have the Holy See support Allied
denunciations of alleged Nazi atrocities was one of the reasons for his
decision, in August of 1942, to send Myron Taylor on a third visit to
the Vatican. But Roosevelt was primarily concerned by the possibility that the Pope's involvement in peace initiatives would undermine
Roosevelt's determination to fight the war until the unconditional
surrender of the Axis powers. Taylor was to impress on the Pope Roosevelt's unshakable resolve in this respect. Taylor's extraordinary trip
through enemy territory to the Vatican was undoubtedly the high
point of 1942 for my father.*

Prior to Mr. Taylor's trip to the Vatican, the United States Government had been primarily concerned about two things: 1) the
effect on the Holy See of Nazi propaganda concerning alleged
Allied plans to curtail religious freedom and 2) reports of
attempts by the Axis to use the Vatican as a medium for a com-

promise peace which would be against the interests of the United States and the Allied powers.

I received a telegram from the Department of State on August 3, stating that enemy propaganda was instilling a dangerous fear in the minds of the people in the unhappy captive nations by reporting the existence of secret agreements among the United Nations allegedly dictated by Soviet Russia that would curtail the future freedom of religious beliefs in Europe were the Allies to win the war. I went to see Cardinal Maglione on August 14, informing him that the United States Government was fully aware of this insidious Nazi propaganda, but Maglione told me that the Vatican was not in the least impressed.

In light of rumors circulating in Rome about alleged German attempts to involve the Vatican in promoting a compromise peace, I had delivered a note on August 8 to Cardinal Maglione emphasizing that the United States would never consider making peace with the Axis powers before having achieved the complete destruction of Hitlerism. Nevertheless, Roosevelt continued to worry about these issues and decided to send Taylor to the Vatican.

On August 22, I received a telegram from Washington advising me of the President's decision, and I immediately requested Monsignor Montini to seek Italian Government permission for Taylor's passage through Italian territory to the Vatican City. Next day Monsignor Montini presented the request formally to the Italian Ambassador to the Holy See, Baron Raffaele Guariglia, and afterwards I received assurance from Montini that he expected a favorable reply from the Italian Government. A few days later, however, Monsignor Montini called me to his office and informed me that, while the Pope would be delighted to receive Taylor, permission for his visit was meeting with unexpected opposition from the Italian Foreign Office, because of the recent refusal of the United States to grant safe sea passage to the Italian Ambassador designate to Buenos Aires. Monsignor Montini added that the Italian Ambassador to the Holy See had suggested that news of the Taylor visit be suppressed in the United States until this problem had been worked out.

In the meantime, Italian Foreign Minister Ciano approved the Taylor visit by ruling that the provisions of the Lateran Treaty, giving accredited diplomats full access to the Holy See, should prevail without reference to the travel problems that the Italian Ambassador to Buenos Aires might be having with the United States. According to a report of the German Ambassador to the Quirinal, it was Mussolini himself who made the final decision. The Apostolic Delegate in Washington advised the President that the Italian Government had given its consent to have Taylor cross the frontier into Italy between the 7th and 20th of September. He added that the Holy See anticipated no further difficulties and that any delay would be attributed to the time necessary for the Italian officials to complete security arrangements.

The Department of State instructed me to find appropriate lodgings for Ambassador Taylor inside the Vatican City, since it would be impossible for him, as a citizen of a nation at war with Italy, to remain in Rome on Italian territory. I consulted my friends in the Vatican Secretariat of State, who at first offered to have one of the elegant suites in the Vatican Palace made ready for him. However, I felt that they preferred to have him stay with me in Santa Marta, where his presence might be less of a problem for the Vatican's neutrality. I consented, but only if a second, fully equipped bathroom were added to our apartment so that Mr. Taylor could have exclusive use of our own, connected as it were to our bedroom, which we expected to turn over to him. This the Vatican agreed to do immediately and everything was completed when Mr. Taylor arrived. Extra furniture was borrowed from D'Arcy Osborne's apartment.

Having relinquished our own bedroom and bathroom to our guest, my wife and I moved to the room previously occupied by my secretary, Miss Flammia, who was able to secure quarters in the main building across the courtyard. We also retained the services of Mario, caretaker of the Alexander Kirk home in Rome, who had served as valet to Taylor during his two previous visits. With this we felt that we had completed preparations to the best of our ability.

Ambassador Taylor left New York for Lisbon by Clipper on September 2. Next day we received news of his safe arrival in the Portuguese capital but learned to our regret that his wife, Annabel, whom we were also expecting, had decided not to make the trip because of the difficulties of wartime travel. On September 17, Ambassador Taylor flew from Lisbon to the Littorio airport north of Rome in an Italian commercial plane. Arriving in the late afternoon, he was welcomed officially by Father Walter Carroll, the American member of the Vatican Secretariat of State, by Monsignor Principi of the protocol division, and by Engineer Galeazzi. I had asked the Vatican Secretariat of State whether the Italian Government would allow me to leave the Vatican City to go to the airport and join the welcoming party, but Monsignor Montini told me that the answer was negative, much to my disappointment. The party was driven without stopping from the airport to the Vatican City in one of the papal limousines, with cars of the Italian security police both leading and trailing.

The morning after Mr. Taylor's arrival, Monsignor Montini came to see me in the living room of our apartment in Santa Marta. He had been sent by the Pope himself, not only to greet our guest but also to find out from him in advance the subjects he intended to bring up in the forthcoming meetings with the Holy Father. But Mr. Taylor was unwilling to see Monsignor Montini at this moment. Exhausted from his trip the day before, and in the midst of digesting the contents of the numerous and often lengthy memoranda prepared for presentation to the Pope, he preferred to remain by himself and undisturbed before his first audience scheduled for the evening of the next day.

Ambassador Taylor was received by the Holy Father on September 19, 22, and 26; he left Rome to return home on September 28. As in 1940 and 1941, Mr. Taylor never invited me to accompany him on his meetings with the Pope. The first audience lasted two hours, the longest ever accorded to a member of a Diplomatic Corps by Pius XII since he had assumed the papacy three years before. Mr. Taylor was always deeply affected by the warmth of the reception he invariably received from His Holiness. One of the ways Mr. Taylor expressed his appreciation for these special attentions was dramatic. Although a Protestant, at first a Quaker and then Episcopalian, he would, before retiring after each audience, never fail to genuflect devoutly before the Holy Father and to ask for and receive the Apostolic blessing as though he were a Catholic.

Four different memoranda were delivered to the Pope by Mr. Taylor, covering six major aspects of United States policy:

a) complete defeat of the Axis powers
b) the Russian question
c) the bombing of Rome and other Italian cities
d) Nazi atrocities
e) postwar material and financial relief for Europe to be provided by the United States, and the preservation of order
f) establishment of a world organization to keep the peace and an international Court of Justice

Although Pius XII had a good command of English, the lengthy documents which Mr. Taylor read to him, containing much diplomatic language, must have caused considerable problems for the Pope. I assume that there was an interpreter present, although I cannot remember who it was. On his return to Washington, Taylor reported that he had finally convinced the Vatican authorities that the U.S. would win the war. Here Taylor was undoubtedly exaggerating, since it became clear to me that once the U.S. had entered the war, the Vatican no longer seriously considered the possibility that the Axis powers would emerge victorious.

Even though 68 years old, Myron Taylor was an indefatigable worker. He would arise at 5 A.M. and work until 8 A.M., when he would eat a hearty breakfast. From then on, he would meet a constant stream of visitors, with spurts of dictating in between. The pace he set left us exhausted, but he continued fresh as a daisy. His visit added interest and zest to our life in Santa Marta.

Mr. Taylor's presence in the Vatican of course came to the attention of the Axis diplomats, who speculated (perhaps through wishful thinking) that the real purpose of his visit was to explore the possibility of peace. It was indeed extraordinary that Taylor was permitted by the Italian Government to travel to the Vatican, particularly since he did not have formal diplomatic status. In fact, Taylor was so impressed by the courtesies extended to him by the Italians that he requested Cardinal Maglione to convey his gratitude and thanks to Foreign Minister Ciano and Mussolini himself. Taylor went so far as to ask Maglione whether he thought it possible to arrange a meeting with the Italian leaders to express his appreciation in person. The Cardinal told Taylor that while the Italian Government would never agree to such a meeting, he would convey Taylor's thanks to the Italian Ambassador to the Holy See. This request

by Taylor was a surprising display of naiveté on his part, unless
he had in mind some Machiavellian ulterior motive.

I subsequently heard from reliable sources that Mussolini
regretted having allowed the Taylor visit, which he viewed as
having been harmful to Italian interests. Roosevelt briefly considered sending Taylor on a fourth visit to the Vatican in 1943,
to make sure that the Pope understood that the Allied invasion
of Italy was not directed against the Italian people or the Holy
See. The idea was quickly abandoned when it became clear that
the Mussolini Government would not permit it. Moreover, the
State Department advised the President that I, as chargé d'affaires inside the Vatican, could adequately handle any problems
arising from hostilities on Italian soil.

The World War II Vatican diplomatic papers, published as Actes et
Documents du Saint Siege, *contain the texts of the various memoranda submitted by Taylor to the Pope during his visit. Besides the
ever-recurring themes that the United States and its allies were certain of their ultimate victory over Nazism and that therefore they
would never accept any compromise peace with the Axis powers,
Taylor's memoranda outlined plans for the reconstruction and reor-
ganization of postwar Europe in which the United States would play
a predominant role. Taylor also repeated Roosevelt's previous views
regarding the mellowing of the Soviet Union as a result of its
alliance with the Anglo-Saxon democracies. Taylor told the Pope
that he believed this would lead to religious freedom in Russia and in
general would bring the Soviet Union into the "family of nations."
Once again, the Holy See was not impressed, as evidenced by Monsignor Tardini's written notations:*

> *This memorandum on Russia demonstrates the error and
> illusion of the Americans, who believe it possible that the*

Communist Government, once victorious, would enter as a gentle little lamb in the European family of nations. The truth is quite different. If Stalin wins the war, he will be the lion which will devour all of Europe. I told Taylor that neither Hitler nor Stalin will be able to remain quiet and calm in a family of European nations. I am amazed that such obvious matters are not recognized by such high level political leaders.

On September 26, Taylor met with Tardini to say goodbye, and the conversation turned once again to the Soviet Union's antireligious policies. Taylor told Tardini that the United States was making every effort to persuade the Russian Government to establish freedom of religion, but Tardini insisted that there was no sign of any change in this respect. Taylor then said it will be necessary for the Soviet Union as well to become part of the family of nations, to which Tardini replied: "Stalin would not be suitable as a member of any family."

Tardini expressed concern not only with the U.S. views on the Soviet Union, but also with Taylor's presentation of the postwar policies of the American Government. In a memorandum reporting on his conversation with Taylor on September 22, Tardini wrote:

In conclusion, I came away from our long talk with the following impressions:

1. *That the US feels strong, is sure of victory and is not afraid of a long war.*
2. *That the US is preparing to reorganize Europe as it deems best. And since hardly any American understands the European situation, this impulse could cause Europe enormous problems.*
3. *That the US, after having reshaped Europe in their fashion, will want to control it and hold it on a leash, so that another war shall not occur.*

All things considered, one must conclude that if National Socialism prepared and provoked the war, the US is itself gravely infected with nationalism, which bodes all kinds of ills and excludes every forecast of good.

It is not clear whether Tardini's skeptical attitude toward United States policies was shared by the Pope and Cardinal Maglione.

During Taylor's visit, the Pope appealed to President Roosevelt to avoid the indiscriminate bombing of civilian populations, stating that the Holy See had made many such appeals in the past to all of the belligerents. The Pope was obviously concerned about the possibility that Rome would be bombed, but his appeal to Taylor was undoubtedly motivated by the recent beginning of large-scale night bombing of Italian cities by the RAF. Taylor claimed that the United Nations would not engage in indiscriminate bombing similar to German attacks on British cities, but admitted that the civilian population would inevitably suffer because of the very nature of aerial bombardment. Taylor stated that he was not clear whether the Holy See had condemned the Axis bombing of various cities, such as London, Warsaw and, curiously, Pearl Harbor, which was not an attack directed at civilian targets. Nevertheless, Taylor undertook to discourage, in London and Washington, indiscriminate bombing and to urge that targets be confined to munitions plants and communications centers.

Taylor kept his word. On his return to the United States from his Vatican visit, he stopped in London and met with Prime Minister Churchill. He asked Churchill to exclude Rome from bombing, but Churchill refused. Taylor then asked Churchill to announce publicly that bombing would be limited to military objectives. Churchill again refused, pointing out that night bombing did not lend itself to accurate bombing of military objectives only, and that night bombing would continue. On his return to the United States, Taylor asked President Roosevelt whether he (Taylor) might inform the Vatican *that the United States would follow an "independent course of action" (from the British) with respect to the bombing of Rome and civilian populations. However, nothing came of this idea.*

On October 5, 1942, a petty officer in the British Navy, A. E. Penny, escaped from an Italian prison camp near Viterbo and bicycled his way to Rome some fifty miles away, penetrating the Vatican City with amazing cleverness and ending in Osborne's apartment. Osborne immediately advised Monsignor Montini that Penny had come into the Vatican City confident of the Pope's protection and expecting that he would be accorded freedom of movement within the Papal domain. It was an embarrassing situation for the Holy See to harbor a military officer of Italy's enemy. Three days later, Osborne was told by Montini that the Italian Ambassador had demanded the immediate surrender of Penny back into Italian hands. The British Minister, however, answered that in his opinion there was nothing in the Lateran Treaty between Italy and the Holy See upon which the Italian demand could be based and warned that he had no intention of giving up the ex-prisoner except under protest in the face of *force majeure*.

Osborne then suggested that the answer might be to arrange for an exchange of Penny for an Italian prisoner in Allied hands. Montini agreed to approach the Italian authorities, but insisted that in the meantime Penny stay within the precincts of the British Legation in Santa Marta and not be seen roaming through the Vatican Gardens to take the air. He was jokingly referred to by other diplomats as the "Military Attaché of the British Legation to the Holy See." Within a few weeks the British and Italian Governments concluded an exchange agreement with the help of the Holy See, so that on January 3, 1943, Penny, accompanied by a Vatican monsignor, flew to Lisbon on

an Italian airliner on his way to London. The same monsignor
escorted the exchanged Italian prisoner on his way back to Rome.

*At the end of 1943 and the beginning of 1944, my father also became
involved in assisting escaped prisoners of war, but the main issue he
faced during the next year and a half would be the Allied air attacks
on Italy in general and on Rome in particular.*

CHAPTER 4

1943

*I*n September 1942, my brother Barclay and I returned to our boarding school in Switzerland on the overnight Rome-Geneva train. The trip was uneventful, as the Royal Air Force raids on northern Italy had not yet reached their highest level of intensity. The sleeping car service was comfortable and hardly seemed affected by wartime conditions. We were undoubtedly the only persons traveling on U.S. passports, on which Italian exit visas had been duly stamped. The Mussolini government, perhaps at the prodding of the Vatican authorities, continued to issue such visas to permit us (and on occasion our mother) to spend our school holidays with our father in the Vatican. We thus returned to the Vatican for the 1942 Christmas vacation and for two weeks during the 1943 Easter break. Prior to the latter trip, my father was told that the Italian authorities were not happy about the number of trips being made by our family members through Italian territory, and were threatening to issue visas only for travel relating to the long summer school holiday. But this threat did not materialize, although we were never certain when, or whether, the visas would be issued. This was particularly true for the trips to Rome from Switzerland, when we had to go to the Italian Consulate in Geneva to have our passports stamped.

When our Christmas vacation in the Vatican ended in January 1943, my mother returned to Swizerland with us and spent three months in Gstaad, the ski resort where our school's winter campus

*was located. She worried about future trips to the Vatican, since the
RAF was stepping up its nighttime raids on Milan, through which
the Geneva-Rome trains had to pass. We often heard the rumble of
aircraft motors at night, as British bombers headed for their Italian
targets. Nevertheless, we were all anxious to rejoin my father, and
my mother decided that we should take the risk for the spring holidays. After an uneventful trip, our family was reunited in the Vatican for Easter.*

*Allied air attacks on Italian cities were of course a major concern
for the Holy See. The Vatican authorities became increasingly worried as the bombing intensified in the early months of 1943. They
were upset by the civilian casualties and damage to church property,
which led to frequent and reproachful representations to my father
and the British Minister, D'Arcy Osborne, as my father recounted in
his memoirs.*

At the end of 1942 and the beginning of 1943, the archbishops of
Milan, Turin, Genoa, Naples, and Palermo had all complained
in letters to the Pope about the heavy Allied air raids on their
cities. The Holy Father replied, "You are not unaware how we
have repeatedly done everything possible to the end that civilian
populations of all countries be spared such atrocious sorrows."
Cardinal Maglione and other Vatican officials had frequently
indicated to D'Arcy Osborne and me that these raids were slowly turning the Italians against the Allies. Osborne felt it the
proper moment to submit a memorandum explaining the
British bombing policy:

1) It was directed only toward weakening the capacity of
   the enemy for continuing the war through the destruction of war-industries, communications and ports.
2) Damage to civilian and ecclesiastical properties was
   inevitable, but never an objective.

3) In two and a half years of war the total casualties among the civilian population for the whole of Italy from aerial bombardments were less than those of a single city such as Warsaw, Rotterdam and Belgrade and probably less than any one of the British cities that suffered bombardments by the Axis. As a matter of fact, the victims in England during the first three months of the blitz (September 8 to December 10, 1940) were 21,668 killed and 30,556 wounded.

4) It was not possible to distinguish between the Italian people who are afflicted by the war, although not responsible for it, and the Italian state, the Fascist government which deliberately and without provocation declared war on Great Britain. The Italian people should blame their government for bringing them into the war and for not protecting them better from its consequences, but not the British people who had no quarrel with them.

5) They should remember that Mussolini, the head of their government and therefore their representative in the eyes of the world, had asked Hitler for permission to participate in the German air attacks on London in the autumn of 1940 which were intended to destroy British morale and thereby defeat the British people.

Osborne also submitted to the Vatican a series of comments appearing during the London blitz in the principal Roman newspapers, *Il Messagero* and *Il Giornale d'Italia*, which gloated over the hardships the British were suffering as a result of the Axis bombardments.

On January 31, 1943, a tragic accident occurred during a daylight raid by the United States Air Force on the harbor installations of the city of Messina in Sicily. A bomb was dropped at this time on a villa near the town of Reggio Calabria situated directly across the Straits of Messina. The Archbishop of Calabria and the Vicar General were both killed outright and there were other victims besides. The Vatican newspaper *l'Osservatore Romano*, in its account of the tragedy, stated that the two unfortunate prelates were at the time on a "pastoral visit" to a social gathering in a private villa. However, strangely enough, Cardinal Maglione did not protest the incident either to me or to my British colleague and we therefore assumed that the gathering was not entirely a social one, but also a meeting of Axis military officials and under the circumstances a legitimate target for Allied bombs. According to a London source, official investigators concluded that the pilot of one of the "Liberator" aircraft engaged in the attack had been obliged to jettison one of his bombs while flying over nearby Reggio Calabria and it was this that had caused the deaths. Whether there was any truth in these explanations or not was never clarified, but the uncertain outcome of an air raid was made even more clear. The Italian press used the incident to launch an intensive campaign to arouse the patriotic feelings of the Italian people and of Catholics everywhere against the Americans.

On April 18, Cardinal Maglione informed me that he possessed "positive evidence" from a "high Italian official" that an American pilot, flying low over the outskirts of Naples, had deliberately machine-gunned civilians, particularly a bus filled with laborers. The Cardinal warned me that, as a result of such incidents, the Americans were beginning to be regarded as less humane than the British. I reported this conversation to the State Department, which instructed me to request the Vatican authorities to furnish details of the machine-gunning such as the exact time and place, the extent of the casualties, names of the victims, and the nature of the "positive evidence" supporting the charges. The Department noted that reports of this nature were often Axis inspired and usually untrue.

Cardinal Maglione also spoke to me about the April 26 American daylight air raids on the town of Grosseto about 190 kilometers north of Rome. He stated that the civilian population had been intentionally machine-gunned from the air and he repeated his warning that Italian opinion was turning against the United States. Also, he mentioned that several aviators who had parachuted during the raid had been roughly handled by an angry crowd. Later Monsignor Tardini told me that the local bishop had visited the American prisoners and had found them unharmed, with no complaints about their treatment. I told Maglione that I felt the atrocity stories from Grosseto to be grossly exaggerated; the Italian authorities at that time were in the midst of an "atrocity" campaign in the Fascist press and on the radio, hoping to rouse the populace out of its lethargy. For instance, *Il Messagero* on April 30, 1943, reproduced on its front page a photograph of Cardinal Spellman of New York conversing and smiling with American aviators in England just before they took off for a daylight raid on Antwerp, then occupied by the Germans, and "massacred the innocent Belgian population." On May 2, the same newspaper published pictures of "explosive pencils and fountain pens dropped on Naples by American airmen," while on May 4, it carried the gruesome photograph of the mutilated body of a baby with a caption stating that the horror had been caused by one of these devices.

On May 6, Washington received a report from the United States representative in Tangier that Mario Badoglio, the son of the Marshal and Italian Minister in Tangier, had mentioned to a Spanish colleague after returning from Rome that the German and Italian governments were discussing the possibility of adopting the Japanese practice of executing Allied aviators who might fall into their hands after the bombing of open towns. Badoglio thought that such action would affect the morale of the Allied pilots, especially when they were ordered deliberately to bomb a "seaside resort" such as Grosseto (actually Grosseto is five miles inland).

On May 20, I had another long conversation with Cardinal Maglione. I should explain that the complaining attitude he displayed is easier to understand in light of Maglione's great affection for his native Italy. The Allied air attacks on his country, especially on his birthplace and home town, Naples, placed him under a high degree of emotional strain. However, I found him in a chastened frame of mind. He admitted that after all he had no proof of the alleged machine-gunning of civilians, that he had erred in ever raising the question, and that he hoped he would be forgiven. He recalled that he had mentioned the raids to me in strict confidence on a purely humanitarian basis and out of regard for the good name the Americans enjoyed in Italy. I told him I was surprised by his insistence that I report the Naples and Grosseto incidents to Washington without his being certain of the facts, for he had assured me all along that he would be careful not to make such charges unless he had positive proof to support them. I added that the Cardinal's action indicated that he himself, as well as other Vatican officials, might have fallen victims to Axis propaganda and that under the circumstances I thought it only fair that he should take immediate steps to dispel any misconceptions in the Vatican regarding the behavior of American airmen. Maglione assured me in the most friendly way that he had already done so and was now certain that Vatican personnel no longer held such notions. This I was relieved to hear.

Later, I saw Tardini and Montini. Both agreed with me that the Naples and Grosseto affairs had been exaggerated in the interests of Axis propaganda, and they confessed that unfortunately the

Vatican had been "taken in," at least temporarily. They did repeat, though, that they still believed that the Americans should always be careful to ensure the safety of Italian civilians. Tardini was happy to tell me that according to the latest reports regarding a second American raid on Grosseto and in a more recent one on Civitavecchia, a port on the Tryrrhenian Sea about 60 kilometers north of Rome, there had been complete success in avoiding all but military objectives. He had also learned that Allied bombings of the airfield and railroad station in Foggia, near the Adriatic Sea, had been very accurate. On May 28, the first American air raid on Leghorn had also been accurate, but during a second raid an orphanage was hit, killing many children.

Vatican officials remained concerned by the havoc wrought on Italian cities. One of them observed to me that the Italian cities, with their industries and tourist attractions, were the only source of wealth which their country possessed. There were no natural resources in Italy such as oil, coal or other minerals which were the basis of prosperity in other lands.

On June 1, I received the following telegram from Washington; it was in reply to my reports:

> The Department shares your surprise that such a high Vatican official as Cardinal Maglione should have been so badly deceived by obvious enemy propaganda in connection with the Naples and Grosseto raids. Not only were the Vatican charges considered important enough in Washington to be forwarded to the Allied Commanders-in-Chief in North Africa for investigation, but also Myron Taylor personally left a memorandum with President Roosevelt on the subject.
>
> While we do not intend to use the Vatican findings for the purpose of replying to the Axis atrocity campaign, it

is obvious that the Cardinal cannot expect to make charges
of so serious a nature "in strict confidence."

The Apostolic Delegate in Washington advised Undersecretary of State Sumner Welles that the Holy See had never placed
any credence in the Axis reports on the use of explosive pens and
pencils by American and British aviators and that the Vatican
newspaper *l'Osservatore Romano* had always refrained from
reproducing any one of the many anti-Allied atrocity stories
appearing in the Fascist press. Cicognani repeated to Welles what
Maglione had already told me, namely that the Vatican possessed
no proofs to support the alleged machine-gunning of civilians.

The Fascist government made a further attempt to create
anti-Allied sentiment among the Italian population. On June
10, the third anniversary of Italy's declaration of war on Great
Britain, an anti-British pamphlet entitled *"Perfida Inghilterra
(Perfidious England)"* was circulated in Italy and the contents
published in the Fascist press. The pamphlet contained a vehement anti-American letter written by the Bishop of Grosseto,
His Excellency Paolo Galeazzi. I protested to both Monsignor
Tardini and Monsignor Montini about the publication of such a
letter by a member of the hierarchy of the neutral Holy See. I
was told that the Vatican deplored the letter and that the guilty
bishop, with his diocese in ruins, must have been under emotional stress when he wrote it. On July 7, the Vatican informed
me that when Bishop Galeazzi had written his letter, he had not
realized that his text would be altered for propaganda use. Vatican officials clearly considered the pamphlet in very bad taste.

*It must have been clear to the Vatican that the best way to spare Italy
from further destruction was the conclusion of a separate peace with
the Allies. My father believed that, in the early months of 1943, the*

Italian Government would welcome such a development and that
the Holy See might act as an intermediary.

There was much speculation among the diplomats in the Vatican City after the appointment of Count Galeazzo Ciano as the new Italian Ambassador to the Holy See on February 7, 1943, after a complete reshuffle of the Fascist cabinet by Mussolini. Ciano had been the Foreign Minister for the preceding seven years, and in view of the unfavorable course the Italian war was taking, it was rumored that the appointment was an attempt by the Italians to begin negotiation with the Allies through the Holy See toward separating Italy from the conflict. Ciano's choice of Marchese Blasco Lanza d'Ayeta, with his close American connections, to be his Counselor of Embassy at the Holy See was also seen as significant.

The fourth anniversary of the Coronation of Pope Pius XII was celebrated in the Sistine Chapel on March 12, 1943, and the entire diplomatic corps attended. Count Ciano was there in a genial mood; with him was his wife Edda, Mussolini's daughter, with flashing black eyes, a magnificent sable cape, and a traditional mantilla over a neat coiffure with two small curls like small horns arising from her forehead. They both exchanged smiles with D'Arcy Osborne and myself.

D'Arcy Osborne went to England on six weeks' leave from April 6 to June 18, during which time he was knighted by the King of England. The Italian Government arranged for his transportation between Rome and Lisbon on Italian commercial aircraft. The Italians' accommodating attitude was in complete contrast to their refusal, early in March 1941, to permit him to attend the funeral of King Alfonso XIII in Rome. This new attitude seemed to indicate an Italian desire to warm up to the British.

R.A.F. night bombers flew over sections of Rome in early May, dropping flares and propaganda leaflets, some of which fell in the Vatican City. It was the first appearance of British planes over Rome since war had been declared three years before. The thousands of leaflets advised the Italians to get out of the war and to accept "peace with honor"; some of the leaflets contained blandishments, others threats: "As long as Italy remains an instrument of Germany, your industrial cities will be bombed without respite . . . Day and night from Benghazi, Tripoli, Malta, Tunisia and Algeria Allied planes will pulverize the ports, railroads, and industrial centers of Italy. Today the war is at the gates of Italy. Peace is within the hands of the Italian people. The choice is up to you! If you still want war, we shall wage a *total war*. Africa is ours. Our naval vessels are able to bombard the Italian coastal cities along a 2,500 mile front. Our soldiers can land anywhere in Italy."

Several days after the British leaflets fell, Cardinal Maglione called Osborne and myself into his office where several of them were spread on his desk. The Cardinal was confident, he said, that the leaflets were only released after the Allied governments had approved of their contents. He asked in particular whether they indicated any softening of the Allied demand for "unconditional surrender" by Germany, Italy, and Japan, a demand made public by Roosevelt with the concurrence of Churchill at the Casablanca Conference on January 24, 1943. "Unconditional surrender" had been regarded, in Europe especially, as a threat of ruin and even annihilation of the Axis countries. Maglione's query, along with several leaflets, were sent to London and Washington on May 20. Both capitals replied that the leaflets meant no change whatsoever in the policy of "unconditional surrender." Maglione stated that the information was for his and the Holy Father's information alone, but both Osborne and I suspected that the Italian Government had inspired his questions. It was the first step known to us taken by the Holy See to act as intermediary in the making of a separate peace for Italy without the humiliation implicit in the Allied policy of "unconditional surrender."

Pope Pius XII himself had been upset by this Allied policy with its vindictiveness and dire implications for Italy's future. On May 18, soon after the leaflets had fallen, the Pope wrote a long personal letter to President Roosevelt, drafted in English and pleading for the protection of Italy:

> As the Episcopal See of the Popes is Rome, from where through these long centuries they have ruled the flock entrusted to them by the divine Shepherd of souls, it is natural that amid all the vicissitudes of their complex and chequered history the faithful of Italy should feel themselves bound more by ordinary ties to this Holy See, and have learned to look to it for protection and comfort, especially in hours of crisis . . . The assurance given to us in 1941 by Your Excellency's esteemed ambassador, Mr Myron Taylor, and spontaneously repeated by him in 1942, that "America has no hatred of the Italian people" gives Us confidence that they will be treated with consideration and understanding; and if they have had to mourn the untimely death of dear ones, they will yet, in their present circumstances, be spared as far as possible further pain and devastation, and their many treasured shrines of Religion and Art—precious heritage not of one people, but of all human and Christian civilization . . . will be saved from irreparable ruin. This is a hope and prayer very dear to our paternal heart, and we have thought that its realization could not be more effectively ensured than by expressing it very simply to Your Excellency. With heartfelt prayer we beg God's blessings on Your Excellency and the people of the United States.

Although the Pope did not specifically mention the Allied policy of "unconditional surrender," he undoubtedly hoped to stress in advance his complete reliance on the friendly feelings of the Americans towards Italy in case that country should be obliged to negotiate a separate peace.

President Roosevelt's reply on June 16 was couched in the most cordial terms. But it was confined to the subject of bombing and was devoid of any mention or reference to "unconditional surrender." Nor did the President give any assurance that Rome would not be bombed:

> The deep feelings of emotion with which Your Holiness views the devastating effects of war on Italy strike a very responsive chord in my heart. No one appreciates more than I the ceaseless efforts of Your Holiness to prevent the outbreak of war in Europe in 1939 and subsequently to limit its contagion. Your Holiness is familiar with the repeated efforts which were made in 1940 by this government, and by many elements within the United States, to deter the Chief of the Italian Government from plunging his country and countrymen into a ruinous war whose outcome, I reminded him even at the time, could only prove disastrous.

At the end of his letter, the President warned the Pope that Axis planes could possibly bomb the Vatican City during an Allied night raid on Rome and then blame Allied planes for an outrage committed by themselves.

A few days later, while Osborne and I were waiting in the antechamber of Cardinal Maglione, the door of the cardinal's office opened and out came Ambassador Ciano. He took the initiative to shake hands with both of us in a most friendly fashion, even though we were his enemies. This seemed like another hint that the Italian Government wanted out of the war, but nothing further developed from this encounter.

Thus the peace "feelers," if indeed they qualified as such, came to nothing, and the Vatican authorities pursued their efforts to safeguard Rome from air attacks.

During the latter part of the month of May, the whole of June, and into early July, the Vatican became increasingly apprehensive regarding Italy's fate. Many attempts were made by the Vatican during this period to ease the situation by appealing both to Washington and to London. Besides the direct exchanges between the President and the Pope, there were numerous communications between the Apostolic Delegate in Washington and Myron Taylor. On May 22, Cicognani wrote to Taylor invoking the help of the American authorities "to spare Rome from the dire consequences of becoming a battlefield."

The Holy See did not, of course, confine its appeals to the Allies alone. The Vatican was aware that

1. many military commands were still in Rome at that time, including Mussolini himself,
2. that both Italian and German officers were circulating in Rome dressed in civilian clothes,
3. that there was an enormous munitions dump at the Acqua Santa Springs only three kilometers from Rome which, if exploded, could cause incalculable damage,
4. that a large array of bombs could easily be seen at the Ciampino airport, and finally
5. that if the Allies should bomb the outskirts of the capital, this would mean that the Axis soldiers camping there would be obliged to move into Rome immediately, creating further military targets.

The Holy See therefore asked the Italian Government for further assurance that both the Italian and German commands were no longer in Rome and that military objectives of all kinds had been removed from the city and its immediate vicinity.

During May and June, Cicognani transmitted several memoranda to the State Department and to Myron Taylor on the subject of Rome. He reaffirmed the Vatican's oft-expressed attitude regarding "the sad eventuality of the bombing of Rome" and repeated that the Holy Father "would be constrained to express a vehement protest against such action" were the bombing to take place. Referring to current rumors in the Vatican that Rome was to be attacked by Allied aircraft on June 10, he quoted Cardinal Maglione's opinion that "the mention of a precise date so close at hand increased the fear that the Eternal City will not be spared the horrors of an aerial attack and that it will not be granted, in the passion of war, that immunity which, on account of its unique character, it would seem to merit." Cicognani requested that the following points be communicated directly to President Roosevelt:

1. In his personal solicitude for the welfare of all peoples, the Holy Father once again leaves in the hands of the President of the United States the fate of the Italian people, and

2. His Holiness has been saddened by the news that the possibility of the bombardment of Rome has not been excluded. In such a hypothesis, which he hopes will never occur, the Holy Father, as he has said before, will be constrained to protest.

President Roosevelt replied to Cicognani on June 29, stating:

I have noted the observations of His Holiness with respect to the possibility of the bombardment of Rome. As in the past, careful consideration has been given to the expressions of opinion of His Holiness. I recently reassured His Holiness with respect to the bombing of the Vatican City. I trust His Holiness will understand that, should the conduct of the war require it, recognized military objectives in and around Rome cannot be ignored. There is no intention to attack or damage non-military objectives or the historic or art treasures of Rome.

On June 26, Myron Taylor received another long letter from Cicognani stating that in the last few weeks the Allied policy regarding Rome had visibly hardened and military necessity was now the determining factor. Cicognani concluded:

> I trust that the Allied governments, even in terms of military necessity, have fully evaluated the import of a solemn and public protest made by the Holy Father, if Rome should unfortunately become the target of Allied bombers. It is a well-founded fear that if all or part of Rome is laid waste by Allied military forces, there will arise not only in Europe and Latin America, but everywhere a troublesome division of spirits, and most certainly a deep-seated antagonism.

In a memorandum dated June 28 by President Roosevelt to Secretary of State Cordell Hull, the President stated that he thought it would be "worthwhile" to advise the Apostolic Delegate in "very polite language":

1. that we fully realize all that the Pope has said about Rome and that we have no desire to destroy any church property or historic monuments,
2. that, nevertheless, because war is war we must recognize that Rome is the center of the Italian Government and

is of definite use to that government in conducting the war against us. This applies also to the fact that many Germans help to run Italy with German staffs located in Rome itself,

3. therefore, in order to be fair and equally just to both sides, we suggest that the Vatican try to have Rome declared an "open city," i.e. that all military installations, activities and personnel of Italy be removed from Rome, together with the use of all railroad facilities in and about Rome for military purposes. This, of course, would require the cooperative consent of the British, but I agree with Myron (Taylor) that it is worthwhile discussing.

What do you think?

Signed, F.D.R.

By coincidence, Archbishop Cicognani wrote to Myron Taylor on the same day announcing the removal from Rome of Axis military facilities. He stated that the Italian Ambassador to the Holy See, on orders from his government, had informed Cardinal Maglione in writing on June 9 that the Italian military commands were in the process of being transferred from the city and that this action was not only in response to the pleas of the Holy See, but also as part of the plan to "decentralize" for national defense purposes. The Italian Government note added that the only military offices remaining in Rome at the time were administrative ones, but that these too, like the Supreme Command and the General Staffs of all military which were already stationed in rural districts, were being removed. Similar steps had been taken in regard to the German liaison offices and these had either followed the respective Italian commands or were about to do so. However, a local garrison necessary for the protection and security of the civilian population would remain in the city.

Archbishop Cicognani's letter then drew an exceptionally gloomy picture of the future safety of the Allied diplomats residing in the Vatican City:

> His Eminence Cardinal Maglione has directed me to make known the sad and dangerous situation in which the Holy See now finds itself. In fact, on several occasions and from various sources, including some newspapers, the Holy See has already been reproached for harboring within the walls of the Vatican the representatives of the United States and of other powers hostile to the Axis. In the event of the bombardment of Rome, there would be considerable probability of an incited or spontaneous uprising of the people, and it would be difficult, if not impossible, for the Holy See to guarantee the security of the Vatican itself and of the diplomatic personnel. Wheresoever the responsibility of such violence might lie, it will readily be conceded that the Holy See does not dispose of adequate means for preventing it . . . His Eminence Cardinal Maglione has taken full cognizance of the possibility that the Vatican City itself may be bombed, either accidentally or deliberately, by one or the other of the contending forces. He is obliged, however, to reassert that in the calm judgment of posterity, the full responsibility would fall upon the Allies if they gave occasion for such a tragic disaster by bombing any part of Rome.

Back in the Vatican, Cardinal Maglione told me on June 26 that he and the Pope had been discussing the fact that an Allied bombardment of Rome might provoke a popular uprising against the diplomats in the Vatican City, regarded by many as "a nest of spies." The Holy See, which had never wanted the diplomats inside the Vatican in the first place, would not, he said, be in a position to give them adequate protection should such an uprising occur. I replied that if the war could be shortened and thousands of lives saved by bombing Rome, the Allies would surely do so despite the risks faced by a few diplomats. Cardinal Maglione then added that he expected to talk with my British colleague along the same lines.

Osborne told me that he planned to make the following points:

1. without the knowledge and consent of the Italian government no such uprising could occur,
2. it would reflect grave discredit both on the Italian government and the Holy See, and
3. it would serve to allay any hesitation to bomb Rome that the Allies might still be harboring.

Osborne went to see the Cardinal on July 1, and His Eminence played down the threat of a possible demonstration against the Allied diplomats after Osborne had expressed his views. The Vatican probably decided to drop the matter after the Cardinal became aware of our reactions. My own impression was that the Cardinal could not have been speaking from conviction and I suspected that he was testing us to ascertain whether such pressure would help Vatican efforts to prevent the bombing of Rome. Osborne and I agreed that popular spontaneous rioting against diplomats in the Vatican could be excluded in case of Allied bombing of military targets.

The Secretary of State for Foreign Affairs, Anthony Eden, instructed Osborne on June 23 to inform the Pope that if the bombing of Rome should become necessary for military reasons, Allied pilots would be given specific orders to prevent any of their bombs falling into the Vatican. Eden added that his government feared that the Axis might simultaneously bomb the Vatican and charge the Allies with this wanton offense, just as President Roosevelt had previously warned the Pope. Maglione did not believe that such a danger existed, having received assurances from both the Italians and Germans. Maglione asked Osborne and myself to remind our governments that the surest way to spare the Vatican was simply to refrain from bombing Rome.

On June 30, the bombing of Rome was discussed in the House of Commons. When Eden was asked whether he had considered the possibility of declaring Rome an "open city" subject to the removal of military installations, he replied that he had made no approach to the Italian government regarding the bombing of Rome and did not intend to make any. "We should not hesitate to bomb Rome, as we have said before, if the course of the war rendered such action convenient and helpful." He reminded his listeners that Mussolini had asked Hitler for the privilege of sharing in the bombing of London "and we have not forgotten that." Finally, Eden said: "It would be in the interests of humanity if Mussolini could only realize that the best thing he could do for himself and for Italy would be for him to accept the Allied 'unconditional surrender terms.'" I reported to Washington that although the Pope was greatly upset by Eden's words, he still refused to believe that the Allies would ever bomb Rome.

On the night of July 4, Allied planes again dropped spectacular red flares and leaflets on Rome, calling on the population to separate its destiny from the Fascist regime. The Allied "war of nerves" warned the Italian people that cities such as Rome might be bombed at any time, giving the Fascists a pretext for continuing their propaganda campaign of hatred toward the United States and England. For instance, "Perfidious Albion" was a term the Fascist media often used when referring to

Great Britain. President Roosevelt was frequently spoken of as "Del'ano" (his middle name was Delano), which in Italian means "of the anus." In a letter addressed to the Holy See, the Italian Government bitterly rejected as "malicious slander" the repeated accusations by the Allies that the Axis was plotting to drop bombs on Rome and even on the Vatican while Allied planes were flying over the city by night, and then charge the Allies with the deed. The letter had also pointed out that the Axis powers had deliberately refrained from bombing Athens and Cairo to avoid damage to these centers of civilization, without demanding a quid pro quo from the Allies.

On July 6, I advised the State Department that the British Minister, under instructions, had informed the Vatican that there was no thought of asking the Italian Government to declare Rome an "open city" in return for Allied assurances that it would not be bombed and that press and radio reports to the contrary were without foundation. Osborne also made it clear that the British Government had no intention of accepting a protest from the Holy Father in case Rome were bombed.

The possibility of gaining for Rome the status of an "open city" had been considered in the past by both the Americans and the British, since the military and political advantages of adopting such a course would have been considerable, assuming satisfactory guarantees could be obtained. They now decided that the time factor ruled out this possibility, because negotiations would have taken weeks or even months, a delay which the Allies could no longer afford, in view of their strategic timetable. When the Holy See had previously informed the Allies of the assurances from the Italian Government concerning the transfer out of Rome of military installations, it had not certified that the transfer had actually taken place. The Cardinal Secretary of State probably did not believe everything that the Italian Government was saying. Nor had the Allies ever received satisfactory evidence from other sources concerning such transfer. On the contrary, Mussolini remained in Rome, undoubtedly continuing to use the city as the political and military capital of Fascist Italy.

On the Axis side, there was opposition in certain quarters to the declaration of Rome as an "open city." The German military authorities in Italy were reportedly against the demilitarization of Rome. Mussolini had developed a strong personal resentment towards the Romans, because of their unpatriotic apathy towards the war, and he was evidently not strongly motivated to protect Rome, which he viewed as the "worst city in Italy." In addition, the politically influential anticlericals did not favor the "open city" idea, particularly since if Rome were to escape bombing through the efforts of the Holy See, the prestige of the Papacy would be immeasurably increased.

On July 10, when the British-American invasion of Sicily began, the Holy See, whose officials were nearly all Italian, realized that it would be facing many months of anguish and sorrow. On the same day, President Roosevelt sent the following message to Pius XII:

Your Holiness:

By the time this message reaches Your Holiness a landing in force by American and British troops will have taken place on Italian soil. The soldiers of the United Nations have come to rid Italy of Fascism and all its unhappy symbols, and to drive out the Nazi oppressors who are infesting her soil.

There is no need for me to reaffirm that respect for religious beliefs and for the free exercise of religious worship is fundamental to our ideas. Churches and religious institutions will, to the extent that it is within our power, be spared the devastations of war during the struggle ahead. Throughout the period of operations, the neutral state of the Vatican City as well as of the Papal domains throughout Italy, will be respected.

I look forward, as does Your Holiness, to that bright day when the peace of God returns to the world. We are convinced that this will occur only when the forces of evil, which now hold vast areas of Europe and Asia enslaved, have been utterly destroyed. On that day we will joyfully turn our energies from the grim duties of war to the fruitful tasks of reconstruction. In common with all other nations and forces imbued with the spirit of goodwill toward men, and with the help of Almighty God, we will turn our hearts and our minds to the exacting task of building a just and enduring peace on earth.

(signed) Roosevelt

The text of the message was immediately released to the press in Washington. A summary was broadcast over the radio and could be heard in Europe on the evening of July 10.

I received the original text in English from the State Department via Bern during the afternoon of July 13 and delivered it forthwith to the Secretariat of State. Monsignor Montini told me that since Cardinal Maglione was out of the Vatican for a few days, a formal reply from the Pope would be somewhat delayed. It was not, in fact, sent to Washington until 10 days later. Meanwhile, Cicognani advised Myron Taylor on July 15 that while the Pope welcomed the President's assurances regarding the safety of churches, the Vatican City, and the Papal domains, he was unable to conceal his regret at finding in the President's message no indication of an explicit intention on the part of the Allies to avoid bombing the Eternal City.

Montini was unhappy about the publication in Washington of a message to the Pope from another chief-of-state without prior consultation and agreement between them. He mentioned that the Pope, who had been working so hard to maintain his strict neutral status in the conflict, had been upset by the publication without his knowledge of an official document addressed to the Holy Father which contained such scathing remarks concerning the Fascists and the Nazis. Cardinal Maglione told me a few days later that the Vatican attitude toward the Roosevelt message was one of "reserve." When I said that I thought it strange that the Vatican newspaper had not published the text of such an important communication from the President of the United States to His Holiness the Pope, he replied that since there had been no agreement on the matter, the Vatican felt no obligation to do so. Besides, he added, such action would not have been opportune since, in spite of the optimistic assurances of the President, no sooner had the message been dispatched from Washington, six or seven churches and religious institutions in Turin and Catania had been destroyed by Allied aircraft on the night of July 12–13. The Italian popular reaction, Maglione explained, would therefore have been contrary to what had been desired by both parties if the message had been published immediately by the Vatican press.

On the other hand, Allied diplomats in the Vatican City had been most enthusiastic on reading the Roosevelt message and especially praised its timeliness.

Since the text of the letter and its immediate release with fanfare in the United States seemed to indicate that Roosevelt was primarily addressing the American public, the failure of the Allied diplomats to recognize that the message was embarrassing to the Holy See is, in retrospect, surprising. The Vatican documents dealing with the Pres-

ident's letter reflect the displeasure of the Vatican. Monsignor Tardi-
ni, in his usual caustic style, commented on my father's remark to
Montini that Roosevelt's message paid great honor to the Holy See:
"Mr. Tittmann may well believe that the text of the message honors
the Holy See, but I don't believe that it bestows much honor on Roo-
sevelt." While my father, good soldier that he was, defended his Pres-
ident's initiative in his discussions with Vatican officials, the tone of
his memoirs hints that he personally was not enthused.

The Vatican's concerns turned out to be well founded. Mussolini was furious when he read the Roosevelt message and threatened to break diplomatic relations with the Holy See. He
claimed that the message demonstrated a certain connivance
between the Pope and the President of a country that hated
Italy. Two days later, however, Mussolini's anger subsided, since
in the meantime, Cardinal Maglione had informed the Italian
Embassy that the Roosevelt letter had been received with little
enthusiasm in the Vatican. Furthermore, Maglione gave new
assurances that the Holy See would continue as before to maintain its strict neutrality.

When the Allies landed in Italy, I remember that Cardinal
Maglione was upset by the invasion of his own country. He hoped
that the British and American commanders understood the magnitude of the ordeal they faced in order to reach Rome. Although
admitting that he was not an expert historian, he believed that no
attempt to conquer Rome from the south along the roads
between the Apennine mountains and the Tyrrhenian Sea had
ever been successful in the past. He mentioned to me that the difficulties had been highlighted in an account he had just finished
reading about Hannibal's failure to capture Rome after his overwhelming defeat of the Roman Army at Cannae in 216 B.C.

After his great victory, Maglione explained, Hannibal prepared for the conquest of Rome, but decided that his soldiers should have a period of rest during the coming winter before continuing their campaign northwards. For their winter quarters he chose Casinum, an impregnable town on the road to Rome. An adjoining mountain almost three thousand feet high with a pagan temple on the summit dominated the countryside and served as a perfect observation post for the defenders. (Casinum is now Cassino and the mountain is now known as Monte Cassino. It has a Christian monastery instead of a pagan temple on its summit.) The brilliant dictator of Rome, Fabius Maximus, fully realized that, should the Carthaginians occupy Casinum, Rome too would fall, as the road from Casinum to Rome was wide open and indefensible. He accordingly sent a secret agent to infiltrate Hannibal's high command, who successfully tricked Hannibal into abandoning Casinum and switching to Capua for his winter quarters. In the meantime, the Roman troops of Fabius Maximus occupied Casinum and the nearby mountain, thus creating an insurmountable obstacle which later restrained Hannibal's army from even attempting to reach Rome via the southern route.

Cardinal Maglione pointed out that the success of the secret agent of Fabius Maximus in keeping Hannibal away from Casinum saved Rome and the rest of Italy from foreign domination. Evidently, the Cardinal foresaw that Cassino might also prove to be a problem for the Allied forces advancing northward and believed they should consider attacking the Axis by way of the Balkans instead.

On July 14, I reported to Washington that based on a recent conversation I had with Cardinal Maglione, the Holy See now seemed less apprehensive that Rome might be bombed. However, on the next day Maglione informed the diplomatic missions accredited to the Vatican located in Rome—Switzerland, Spain,

Argentina, Chile, Ireland, and Portugal—of the increasing danger they faced from air attacks.

Our two sons, Harold, aged 14, and Barclay, aged 11, arrived by train from Switzerland during the late afternoon of Saturday, July 17, to spend their usual summer vacation with us. Their arrival was delayed many hours because of frequent air alerts along the way. The railroad stations in Milan and Bologna were, in fact, attacked by Allied planes during the trip, but luckily their train had already pulled out from both stations before the bombs fell. My wife became increasingly worried as the train failed to arrive in Rome on schedule and news of the bombings of Milan and Bologna continued to come in over the radio. She now felt that it was pure folly to have arranged for our children to travel through Italy at this time. The boys themselves had not been at all frightened and had slept soundly in their wagon-lits compartment.

On the night of July 18, anti-aircraft fire could be heard as British planes flew over Rome, this time dropping leaflets warning the population that the Eternal City would be bombed the next day. The leaflets assured the Italians that military objectives only, such as railroad stations, freight yards, and airfields, would be the targets and that the crews of the bombers had been especially trained to drop their bombs with the utmost accuracy. The population was urged to stay clear of military targets in the interest of their own safety.

The British planes began to appear at midnight and the last one left the Rome area at nearly three o'clock in the morning of July 19. Despite the late hour, our family went down into the courtyard of Santa Marta to view the extraordinary spectacle. Guns could be heard from every direction as the anti-aircraft batteries opened up, while red rocket flares and tracer bullets streamed brilliantly across the sky. Whenever the din faded, we could hear the voices of the Santa Marta nuns as they prayed continuously in their chapel, which they always did during air raids. The diplomats were advised by the Vatican authorities to take shelter in the basement of the Canonica building next to Santa Marta as soon as an alarm was sounded. However, we could never resist the temptation to watch from the open court-yard rather than taking refuge in the gloomy environment of the Canonica basement, where coffins of former canons of St. Peter's awaited permanent burial elsewhere. We were all confident that the Vatican City itself would continue to be spared.

During the morning of July 19, I visited Monsignor Montini in his office to report the safe arrival of our two sons. Suddenly, we heard a burst of anti-aircraft fire and Montini asked me whether I wished to go to the shelter, especially since his office was in an exposed position on the top floor of the Vatican Palace. I replied that I was willing to follow whatever he did. He then declared that he never took shelter during air-raid alarms, as he did not believe that Rome, much less the Vatican City, would ever be bombed by the Allied air forces. He explained that the Holy Father himself and many of his closest advisers, including Monsignor Tardini, felt the same way. In view of Monsignor Montini's confident attitude, we continued our conversation without moving from our chairs. I learned later that Pius XII had been relying on soothing reports from Archbishop Spellman, who maintained close contact with President Roosevelt.

Moments later, an usher rushed in from the hallway and excitedly announced that Rome was being bombed and that we had better come out on the Loggia di Raffaello, an open-air gallery in the Papal Palace, to see for ourselves. Upon arriving on the Loggia, we found a small group of youthful prelates and other members of the Vatican Secretariat of State watching the scene in shocked silence.

From the Loggia we could see, across the rooftops of Rome,

a curtain of dust and smoke rising above what we later learned was the San Lorenzo district within the boundaries of the city. At that point, Montini and I were not convinced that the targets were as near as the San Lorenzo freight yards. We believed them to be the airfields outside of Rome, so when we returned to Montini's office, he displayed great relief that the city of Rome itself was not under attack, and we continued our conversation another fifteen minutes amidst the crackle of bursting anti-aircraft shells.

As I left Montini's office, I went out on the loggia again in time to witness one of the younger monsignori, who had been watching the raid, raise his hands on high in a gesture of battlefield leadership, shouting, *Non fa niente. Vinceremo—forse non adesso, ma nel futuro.* (Never mind. We will win—maybe not now, but in the future.) The astonishment and awe of these Vatican onlookers when the raid first began was already beginning to give way to patriotic anger—an indication of the persistent Italianate character of the Vatican staff.

I passed the next hour or so in the company of an American Carmelite monk, watching the bombing as we stood together in the courtyard of San Damaso, where we were protected from falling shrapnel. Later, during a lull in the anti-aircraft fire, I made my way home on foot, arriving at Santa Marta in the early afternoon as the last bombs were being dropped. I then learned for certain that Rome itself had been bombed, with considerable loss of civilian lives, and that the Papal basilica of San Lorenzo had been badly damaged.

Thus a historic event had occurred: Rome had been bombed by the Allies for the first time. A major raid of 500 American bombers, with fighter escorts, started at 11 A.M. and ended at 1:30 P.M.—two and a half hours of agony. Besides the San Lorenzo freight yards, other railroad facilities and airfields were attacked. Over one thousand tons of bombs were dropped and only one American bomber was lost.

At Santa Marta, I found my wife and two boys together with a number of our diplomatic colleagues on the roof-terrace of the main building from where the view of the air activities in progress was excellent. We could see black clouds of smoke billowing up from three directions and a dense pall hovered over the whole city. We could even smell the smoke.

After arriving at the Vatican in July 1943, I began keeping a diary of notable events. This is my description of the July 19 raid:

> *At about a quarter past eleven in the morning, we heard a droning of planes. Suddenly the alarm sounded and the flak opened up simultaneously. We grabbed our field glasses and rushed downstairs. We could see puffs of smoke as the anti-aircraft shells exploded, and then we saw the planes. They were wonderful to see. Flying in perfect formations of three, they swept toward their objectives, gleaming in the bright sunlight.*
>
> *The anti-aircraft defenses made a lot of noise but were completely ineffective. They always seemed to be shooting behind the planes. Then we climbed to the top floor of the Palazzo Santa Marta and looked out of a window. We had at first thought that they were bombing places around Rome, but when we saw huge clouds of smoke rising in the direction of the station, we knew that it was Rome's turn to suffer the horrors of war.*

I obviously viewed the raid with a strong feeling of patriotic pride befitting a fourteen-year-old American boy. I remember some of our diplomatic friends (probably the Poles and the Yugoslavs)

*cheering as the American planes attacked their targets, and D'Arcy
Osborne, from whose apartment we were watching the drama,
expressing his distaste for what he called their "atta boy-ish" excla-
mations. D'Arcy loved Rome, and although he officially supported
his government's resort to saturation bombing of Axis cities, he was
appalled by the destruction and loss of civilian lives that ensued.*

Except for the basilica of San Lorenzo, the nearby Verano ceme-
tery, several university buildings, and a hospital which were hit
by mistake, the bombs all landed squarely on military objectives. According to first reports, over 700 civilians were killed
and 1500 injured, mostly from working-class areas, mainly
because of an unfortunate concentration of crowded streetcars
in the square before the entrance of the basilica of San Lorenzo.

Pius XII, of course, had always hoped that Rome would not
be bombed. He was bitterly disappointed, especially because he
believed the bombing of Rome was unnecessary to force Italy
out of the war. To carry out his pastoral duties as Bishop of
Rome, the Pope, accompanied only by Monsignor Montini, left
the confines of the Vatican City for the first time since Italy had
entered the war three years before and drove to the basilica of
San Lorenzo. His face pale with grief, he stood up in his car to
contemplate the damaged basilica, and then he walked in the
street to mingle with his flock. The Pope knelt down in the rub-
ble and prayed for the victims of this and other raids. Then he
intoned, in a voice that everyone present could hear, the "De
Profundis," the penitential psalm recited during prayers of the
dead. He had also brought with him a supply of lire for the
Capuchin monks of San Lorenzo for distribution by them to
the families who had suffered most from the bombs.

The next day the Pope addressed a letter to the Vicar of Rome,
Cardinal Machetti Selvaggiani. According to tradition, such a

communication is dispatched by the Bishop of Rome to his Vicar each time a catastrophe occurs in the Eternal City, and its contents are published immediately in *l'Osservatore Romano*. The letter was regarded as a substitute for the "public protest" the Pope had been threatening to make over the bombing of Rome. The following excerpt from the letter to the Cardinal Vicar implied that the Axis should share the guilt for the bombing of Rome because of the failure to remove military targets from the city:

> To us it seemed only legitimate that our attitude in the war would have procured for us, amid so much bitterness, the comfort of finding *in both belligerents* a welcome for our efforts in behalf of the safety of Rome. But unfortunately such a reasonable hope ended in disillusionment. What we feared so much as a result of bombing is now a sad reality, because one of the most important Roman basilicas—San Lorenzo outside-the-walls—is now for the most part destroyed.

Osborne and myself regretted that Pius XII had failed to raise his voice in some such manner as this when civilians, cultural monuments, and churches in Great Britain were being bombed by the Germans in the early stages of the war. We felt that although the letter to the Cardinal Vicar may not have been technically a protest, it was nevertheless too pointed. In our opinion, the Pope's visit to the devastated areas was a sufficient gesture; to have written the letter as well was unnecessary.

L'Osservatore Romano of July 24 and 26 carried texts of messages of sympathy received at the Vatican from cardinals, bishops, laymen, and groups in many parts of the world, including Spain, Latin America, and Ireland. No telegrams, however, were received at the Vatican from the British or American hierarchies.

Fascist propaganda was extremely violent and abusive, exploiting the raid to the utmost to turn world Catholic opinion against the Allies. But many of the Fascists were no doubt "shedding crocodile tears." They were pleased that the Papacy had, in spite of constant appeals from the Holy Father, proved itself incapable of protecting Rome, thus suffering a loss of prestige which would strengthen their position.

President Roosevelt discussed the bombing of Rome at a press conference on July 23. He asserted that it was a military necessity in order to save the lives of Allied soldiers in the Sicilian campaign, because Rome was a vital railroad and air communications link between the north and south of Italy. He added that the Allied governments had tried hard to get Rome declared an "open city," but that so far the Axis had prevented this.

Osborne and I had made it a point to avoid appearing at the Secretariat immediately after the raid, fearing that our presence there might be misconstrued as a desire on our part to condole with the Vatican. I finally visited the Cardinal Secretary of State on July 24; I found him unhappy but resigned about the raid on Rome, saying he hoped it would not be repeated. I could give him no assurance on this, since Rome continued to be a transit center for the Axis. Maglione also remarked that he considered the bombing a political mistake. To this I made no reply. I said that I regretted the loss of civilian lives and the damage to the basilica of San Lorenzo, but I explained that the raid had been a military necessity. I also made it clear that I blamed the Italian authorities, forewarned of the raid, for not evacuating the population from neighborhoods with such obvious military targets as freight yards and airfields.

Referring to the Pope's letter to the Cardinal Vicar of Rome, Maglione described it as a "lament" (the Pope was extremely sad) meant for the ears of both belligerents and not as a "protest" against one side only. I answered that I understood this, but that I thought it unfortunate that the letter should have lent itself so readily to Axis propaganda. The Cardinal concluded by saying that the raid had proven the thesis always upheld by the Holy See, that in spite of all the goodwill on the part of attacking air forces, it was impossible to bomb military objectives in Rome without damaging Vatican property or cultural monuments. I replied that the best answer to this was that military objectives should be removed from the city.

Two days later I repeated to Monsignor Montini that I personally deplored the loss of life and the damage to church property resulting from the American raid. He indicated that the Vatican felt hurt because Osborne and I had not expressed these sentiments to the Holy Father through the Cardinal immediately after the raid instead of waiting to do so for almost a week. I pointed out that Axis propaganda had in fact invented a visit by me to Cardinal Maglione immediately after the raid, with the implication that Maglione had protested to me, and that the Vatican radio had been obliged to broadcast a denial. Monsignor Montini replied that he understood our position, but felt that we might have at least sent a personal word of sympathy directly to the Holy Father, who had been bitterly disappointed by our silence.

The Vatican radio, in its German-language broadcast on July 24, replying to the Axis propaganda just mentioned, declared that

1. the Pope had not sent a personal protest to Roosevelt,
2. the American Chargé d'Affaires had not been summoned to the Secretariat of State,
3. the Pope did not say in his letter to the Cardinal Vicar of Rome that the Basilica of San Lorenzo had been completely demolished,
4. the Pope did not question the good faith of the American aviators in their efforts to spare Vatican property, and

5. the Vatican believed it would have been possible to make Rome an "open city" if the Germans and Italians had only cooperated.

Monsignor Montini assured me that these statements, while not official, correctly reflected the Vatican's views.

I suggested to the Department of State that, in view of the rather heavy loss of civilian life, the damage to San Lorenzo, and the Pope's unhappiness, consideration might be given by the United States Government to sending some word of encouragement to the Holy Father. There was no reaction to my suggestion.

The Pope chose to reply to Roosevelt's letter of July 10 on the evening of July 19 after the first bombardment of Rome, and after his visit to San Lorenzo. With no intention of making the contents public, he could use much stronger language than in his communication to the Cardinal Vicar. Although the Vatican did not regard it as a protest against the bombing of Rome, but rather as a repetition of the Holy Father's private appeals to the President, it nevertheless sounded very much like a protest:

Moved by Our strong insistent love for human kind, We cannot but take this occasion of the message which Your Excellency has kindly addressed to Us, to repeat an appeal made by Us more than once in these past few years. It is a prayer that everywhere, as far as humanly possible, the civilian populations be spared the horrors of war, that the homes of God's poor be not laid in ashes, that the little ones and youth, a nation's hope, be preserved from all harm—how Our heart bleeds when We hear of helpless children made victims of cruel war—and that churches dedicated to the worship of God and monuments that enshrine the memory and masterpieces of human genius be protected from destruction. We repeat this appeal unwilling to yield to any thought of its hopelessness, although almost daily We must continue to deplore the evils against which We pray. And now even in Rome, parent of western civilization and for the well-nigh two thousand years the center of the Catholic world, to which millions, one may risk the assertion of hundreds of millions, of men throughout the world have recently been turning their anxious gaze, We have had to witness the harrowing scene of death leaping from the skies and stalking pitilessly through unsuspecting homes striking down women and children; and in person We have visited and contemplated with sorrow the gaping ruins of that ancient and priceless Papal basilica of Saint Laurence, one of the most treasured and loved sanctuaries of Romans, especially close to the heart of all Supreme Pontiffs and visited with devotion by pilgrims from all countries of the world. God knows how much We have suffered from the first days of the war for the lot of all those cities that have been exposed to aerial bombardments, especially for those that have been bombed not for a day, but for weeks and months without respite. But since Divine Providence has made Us head of the Catholic Church and the Bishop of this city so rich in sacred shrines and hallowed, immortal memories, We feel it Our duty to voice a particular prayer and hope that all may recognize that a city, whose every district, in some districts every street, has its irreplaceable monuments of faith or art and Christian culture, cannot be attacked without inflicting an incomparable loss on the patrimony of Religion and Civilization . . .

At the end of his letter the Pope expressed his doubts on the principle of unconditional surrender, which he felt would leave a legacy of hatred. He did not refer to this directly, but it was implied when he said that peace "will stand and endure only if set on the foundation of Christian, more than mere human, charity, not alloyed with vindictive passion or any elements of hate."

On July 25, the Fascist Grand Council, meeting in Rome, deposed Mussolini, confiding the destinies of Italy to King Victor Emmanuel III. The King appointed Marshal Pietro Badoglio as head of state, who immediately proclaimed that the war would continue and that Italy would not forsake her German ally. Mussolini was arrested and imprisoned in a remote mountain location in central Italy. The Roman population reacted with joy and staged numerous anti-Fascist demonstrations. This sudden change in the Italian political situation would become the principal subject of my father's reporting to the State Department during the next few months. He became, in the true sense of the expression, a "listening post" with regard to developments in Italy.

The day after Mussolini's overthrow, several of us from Santa Marta went to watch the gathering crowds in St. Peter's Square, who were no doubt hoping the Holy Father might address them. But nothing happened, as Pope Pius XII had not yet had time to make up his mind what the Vatican attitude should be in face of the sudden shift in Italian politics. In any event, the Holy See traditionally did not comment on internal governmental questions.

Badoglio's words, "The war continues," meant that Italy was not yet ready to surrender to the Allies. Badoglio explained later that he and the King hesitated in the beginning to break completely with Germany because they feared that the Germans would immediately occupy Rome and arrest the King, along with members of the Italian Government. In addition, they still had hopes that the Germans might be persuaded to withdraw their armed forces from the whole of Italy and thus allow the country to become a neutral area.

The Holy See moved immediately to establish friendly relations with the new Badoglio government. The Vatican overtures were naturally welcomed by the government at this crucial moment. Baron Raffaele Guariglia, who had been appointed Foreign Minister on his return from Turkey on July 29, was anxious to keep in close personal touch with Cardinal Maglione. They had established a warm personal friendship during Guariglia's year as Italian Ambassador to the Holy See, and Guariglia developed much respect for Maglione's understanding of international affairs. While the Badoglio government remained in power, Foreign Minister Guariglia often went alone and in complete secrecy to the Vatican, there to discuss with Maglione Italy's ever worsening situation.

Despite Marshal Badoglio's assertion that the war was still going on, Osborne and I felt that we should follow the advice of the Holy See and convince our own governments that Badoglio's strategy was not pro-German as the Allies suspected. During the next month, I sent a series of messages to the Department of State in Washington on the subject. The day after Mussolini fell, I called on Cardinal Maglione to ascertain the reaction of the Holy See to this momentous change. Although the Cardinal displayed his usual reticence regarding Italy's domestic policies, I surmised that the Holy See was not at all unhappy at the collapse of the Fascist regime. I telegraphed the following impressions to Washington:

1. The Fascist Party had voted itself out of office and had thus committed suicide. This was regarded as more satisfactory than if Mussolini had been evicted by another

political party or by the military, because it would prevent any possible revival of the Fascist Party. Throughout the city, the people were joyfully taking part in the liquidation of all Fascist organizations.

2. King Victor Emmanuel III, by calling upon Badoglio to form the new government, had strengthened the Marshal's political position for the time being. However, Badoglio eventually would have to be dropped, since he had been too closely identified with Fascism in the past.

3. The attitude of the Germans was the key, but presently unknown, factor. The statement of Badoglio that the war was still going on was a temporary expedient designed to gain time. The popular demand for peace was overwhelming and would have to be satisfied as soon as possible. The Allies, therefore, should pay close attention to developments in Italy and be ready to intervene in case of German reprisals or public disorders. Allied armed forces would meet with little opposition if they attempted to land on the peninsula and this would be the best way to bring the war to an early conclusion.

4. I believed that the Allies should not bomb Rome again or other populous Italian centers, at least until the new government had time to establish its authority. The Allies should attempt to strengthen the Badoglio government by not saddling it with the odium of partial responsibility for further civilian tragedies resulting from air attacks.

5. Cardinal Maglione repeatedly expressed to me in no uncertain terms his hope that the Allies would show patience and understanding towards the new Italian government.

The prospect of Italy's unconditional surrender to the Allies was less of a preoccupation to the Badoglio government than the uncertainty of German intentions. Vatican officials were closely following all Allied pronouncements relating to the surrender of Italy and were on the lookout for anything that might imply "terms." On August 3, I reported the general feeling in the Vatican that the possibility of German political control of Italy had become so real that the position of the Badoglio government was now very precarious. Completely lacking in aviation and modern arms, the Italian forces were not considered capable of opposing German military occupation of Rome. An early Allied landing would be desirable and if this could be accomplished in the north of Italy, the Germans would be obliged to retire immediately from the south and center of the country. Also, the goodwill of the Italian people toward the Allies was evident and advantage should be taken of this state of mind.

A few days later I informed Washington that the Badoglio government would like to sue for peace without further delay, but was held back by the Nazi threat. Badoglio was obliged, therefore, to play for time in the hope that the Allies would be able to come to the assistance of the Italians with aircraft and a landing on the peninsula, preferably in the north. Only in this way could the Italians expect to oppose successfully any German move against them. Badoglio was not playing the Germans against the Allies in the hope of obtaining better terms from the latter, but was motivated solely by fear of the Germans. Hitler was in a vengeful mood and was seeking a pretext to take over Italy. In order not to risk undermining Badoglio's authority, I urged that the Allies should cease attacking the Marshal in the press or on the radio and refrain from bombing civilian populations.

On August 12, I reported on the current situation in Rome, noting in particular Badoglio's belief that if the Italians tried to surrender to the Allies and the Germans found out about the attempt, the Nazis would seize Rome within two hours. The

Vatican believed that the danger of social disorders now existed and that indiscriminate bombings by the Allies, if continued, could lead to public protests and demonstrations, very likely fomented by the Communists. Although the attitude of the Communists in Italy at that time was uncertain, it was nevertheless known that they were well organized, not without financial resources, and even to some extent armed. If such disorders should take place and the stability of the Badoglio government threatened thereby, the Germans would be presented with one of the pretexts they were seeking to occupy Italy and reinstate the Fascist regime or something even worse. I had been told on good authority that Rome was then surrounded by both Italian and German armed forces, the Germans forming an outer ring and the Italians an inner, the latter drawn up to protect the capital in case the Germans attempted to move in.

In my seventh and last telegram in this series, dated August 22, I reported that according to Cardinal Maglione, the Badoglio government was prepared to conclude an armistice with the Allies as soon as possible, but was still holding back because of the presence of the Germans, who were being steadily reinforced. It considered a military intervention by the Allies as essential. If this were possible, Badoglio would continue to play for time as best he could.

Despite the uncertain political situation, the Allied diplomats continued their usual Tuesday and Thursday jaunts to Fregene, a most welcome diversion in the hot August weather. My family found the trips exciting. Traveling along the Via Aurelia they would meet scores of southbound German vehicles. The German army had set up a camp in the Fregene pine forest, and towards the end of August stationed artillery pieces near the beach. They took down all of the cabins on the beach, apparently because they were in the line of fire of the artillery, so that the visitors from the Vatican City had to change their clothes in the privacy of their automobiles. German soldiers were often encountered relaxing on the beach. The last trip to Fregene was on September 2.

During the early weeks of the new Italian government, while Osborne and I were trying to keep our governments informed, Badoglio was taking steps to contact the Allies, first through the Holy See and then more directly through his own diplomatic and military channels.

Around six in the evening on July 30, I was summoned to the office of the Cardinal Secretary of State. Maglione was seated behind his desk as usual, but in one corner of the spacious and luxurious room with its lovely view of Rome, a man was lounging on a sofa, glancing at us with a friendly smile. Much to my surprise it was none other than Francesco Babuscio Rizzo, the Chief of Cabinet of the Foreign Minister (two days later he would be appointed the Italian Chargé d'Affaires at the Holy See). He was, of course, technically my enemy. The Cardinal, after introducing us, left the room.

Babuscio explained that the reason for our meeting was the Italian government's desire to contact the United States government to begin negotiations for an armistice with the Allies. He said that his government felt that the quickest and more secure channel for this purpose was through the Vatican. He then asked me whether I would be willing to send this information on to Washington but, of course, he insisted on the utmost secrecy. I replied that unfortunately I had no confidential code available and therefore regretfully could not comply with his request. Babuscio said that he too was sorry, but understood perfectly. Maglione, returning to hear the results of the unusual confrontation, was obviously disappointed by the negative outcome.

I later learned that the Cardinal had arranged a similar meeting in his office that same evening between Osborne and Baron Raffaele Guariglia, the newly appointed Foreign Minister. Guariglia posed the same question about Italy's getting in touch with the Allies, but the British Minister also was obliged to refuse. The Italians had broken the only secret cipher the British Legation possessed and Osborne believed that the enemy was reading everything that he was sending out by cable or radio.

Shortly after the meetings we had in Maglione's office, the British Legation received a new secret code in time to report Italy's interest in withdrawing from the war. Washington never gave me one, which disappointed the Holy See and myself, as the United States thereby lost this unique opportunity to participate in the first step toward a peace between Italy and the Allies.

After the failure of the Badoglio government's efforts to approach the Allies through Vatican diplomatic channels, Badoglio sent a number of emissaries to Madrid and Lisbon to negotiate terms for Italy's withdrawal from the war with Allied diplomatic and military officials. My father did not play a direct role in these discussions, which eventually led to the September 8 armistice.

There were no definite signs that either the Americans or the British had been acting on the information and suggestions that Osborne and I had been sending to Washington and London, trying to convince the Allies of Italy's vulnerable position and her readiness to join the Allies. However, by August 25, King Victor Emmanuel and the Badoglio government were less criticized in the Allied press and on the radio, one change in Allied policy traceable to Osborne's and my efforts.

The Holy See used the disappearance of the Fascist regime as an opportunity to renew its previous efforts to have Rome declared an "open city." The Vatican sent an appeal to this effect to the new Badoglio government on July 26, the day after Mussolini's arrest. On July 29, the newly designated Chargé d'Affaires to the Holy See, Babuscio Rizzo, told the Cardinal Secretary of State that the Badoglio government was examining favorably the possibility of declaring Rome an "open city," but that serious difficulties existed independently of the military problem, although there was hope they could be overcome. Three days later, he confirmed the intentions of his government and Foreign Minister Guariglia personally asked Maglione to ascertain what conditions would be necessary for the Allies to recognize Rome as an "open city." Maglione immediately transmitted the above questions to both the British and American governments through the Apostolic Delegates. As a result, the War Department in Washington drew up a list of seven conditions relating to the "open city" question. After Roosevelt's approval they were sent to the British Embassy to be forwarded to London. Maglione, in the meantime, kept me informed at the Vatican of what was taking place.

Churchill advised Roosevelt that he was not inclined to approve any plan containing conditions drawn up by the Allies which the Italian government would be obliged to fulfill. He feared that such a move might be regarded as an abandonment of the principle of "unconditional surrender." While agreeing with the Prime Minister's objections, the War Department nevertheless recommended against an outright refusal to the request of the Holy See. Accordingly, the State Department advised the Apostolic Delegate that "there is nothing to prevent the Italian Government from undertaking unilaterally to declare Rome an 'open city.'"

In spite of the diplomatic exchanges between the Holy See and the United States then taking place in Washington, Rome was bombed for the second time on August 13 from 11 A.M.

until 12:45 P.M. by 278 American aircraft. The targets were again the San Lorenzo and Littorio freight yards. The bombing was more accurate than before, and the civilian casualties were far less. However, many buildings of all kinds and one church were razed. The diplomats of Santa Marta, including of course our two sons, gathered again on the roof-terrace of the palazzo to watch the bombing, which was not nearly as spectacular as the first raid. There was little or no anti-aircraft fire, neither Italian nor German fighter planes could be seen attacking the American bombers, and it was more difficult to pinpoint the targets that were hit since the bombing generated little smoke.

As soon as the all-clear signal was sounded, the Holy Father again carried out his pastoral duties and visited the bombed area in his automobile. The Pope's visit to the bombed areas after the first raid was popularly regarded as a protest against the bombing of Rome; after the second, it was considered by the people merely as a manifestation of the Holy Father's interest in his own diocese of Rome. He was now enjoying unprecedented popularity both in the capital and elsewhere in Italy. There were several demonstrations in St. Peter's Square when cries of "peace" could be heard and during which the Pope appeared on his balcony to give his blessing to the masses below. Full credit was also being given to the American aviators for the precision with which they carried out their mission in the second raid.

Osborne went to see Cardinal Maglione on August 14 following the second bombardment of Rome. Maglione told him that the Allies should not have dropped bombs on Rome while negotiations sponsored by the Holy See were proceeding on the "open city" question. On his return to Santa Marta, Osborne noticed the portico of St. Peter's, the Bernini Colonnade, filled with pathetic women and children camping there for protection in anticipation of another raid which, according to rumors, was due on that day between 10 A.M. and 4 P.M. This depressed him no end and he told me that for the moment he could think of nothing else but the tragic situation of Italy. He was also disturbed over the Allied air attacks on Milan, Turin, and Genoa of August 7, understood to have been the heaviest of the war. In all these raids, churches, cultural, and charitable institutions, many of which were important, were hit, and there were considerable civilian casualties. Osborne sent two long telegrams on August 18 to the British Foreign Office in London protesting the indiscriminate bombing of Italian cities by the Allies. He felt that the Allies were descending to the Nazi level of deliberate "coventrization." He realized, of course, that his views might not be well received in London, but explained to me that he had by his speaking out at least eased his own conscience.

Cardinal Maglione sent long letters to both D'Arcy and me on August 15 deploring in strong terms the two Allied air attacks on Rome. He insisted that further talks take place with the greatest possible speed to resolve the "open city" question, urging that, in the meantime, any further bombings be avoided. The same pleas were made to the British and American governments by the representatives of the Holy See in London and in Washington. Maglione was particularly upset by the latest raid, since the Italian government had notified both the Americans and the British of its intentions to declare Rome an "open city."

Alarmed by the implications of the second bombing of Rome by the Americans, the Badoglio government resolved to wait no longer for replies from the Allies, but instead to follow the American suggestion of a unilateral "open city" declaration. The official communiqué, issued on Saturday evening, August 14, and brought to the attention of the British and American governments through neutral diplomatic channels two days later, stated: "Since July 31 the Italian government had let it be known through the Holy See that it had decided to declare Rome an 'open city' and was expecting to learn the conditions under which this declaration could be accepted. In view of the succeeding air attacks on Rome, the center of Catholicism, the Italian government has determined to proceed, without further procrastination, with the formal and public declaration of Rome 'open city' and is taking the necessary steps according to the norms of international law to make the declaration effective." On August 16, the Italian military command ordered, in the event of future Allied air activities over Rome, the cessation of air defense measures around the city, such as anti-aircraft fire and the use of fighter planes. The news of this decision was conveyed by the Vatican to D'Arcy and to me. On the evening of August 21, while Allied planes were again over Rome dropping propaganda leaflets and taking photographs of objects illuminated by flares, anti-aircraft batteries were silent, no searchlights appeared in the sky, and no fighter planes took to the air.

On August 20, the Holy See informed the Italian government that the Allies would not recognize its "open city" declaration unless Rome were completely demilitarized, including the removal of all means of transportation of troops and military supplies. The Vatican also suggested to the Italians that a neutral Swiss national be called upon to confirm to the Allies that all the necessary measures were being taken. Badoglio accepted the suggestion and immediately got in touch with the Swiss government, but the results were negative as Switzerland did not wish to become involved.

The German government agreed with Badoglio's Rome "open city" policy provided it would not interfere with Axis military supply lines from the north of Rome to the south and that the defenses on the perimeter of the city would not be weakened. On August 23, the German Ambassador to the Holy

See, Baron von Weizsaecker, told Babuscio Rizzo that he was surprised by the dilatory tactics of the Anglo-Americans regarding the implementing of a Rome "open city" policy and that he believed the enemies of Germany wished, in this way, to throw the onus of refusal onto the Axis. Weizsaecker promised to recommend to Berlin that the "open city" idea be accepted, but felt that some public announcement assuring the continuation of the Italo-German solidarity should be made at the same time. Babuscio Rizzo, in his talk with the Ambassador, inferred that controlling railroad traffic (that no trains should be halted within the city) would be most difficult for the Axis to carry out.

Meanwhile, the Intra-Ministerial Committee set up to supervise the demilitarization of Rome with Badoglio presiding had met on August 19 and ordered the immediate removal from Rome of all possible military objectives, both personnel and materiel. Military railroad trains (30 to 40 per day) passing through Rome were forbidden to stop in the "open city." The Italian government provided me, through Vatican channels, with a map indicating the limits of the "open city," which I sent on to Washington by diplomatic pouch.

However, nothing ever came of Badoglio's efforts, enthusiastically supported by the Vatican, to preserve Rome from bombardment. The Allies, in spite of President Roosevelt's sympathy for the Holy See, decided to leave full liberty of action to their military commanders in the field, while the Germans persisted in refusing to relinquish Rome as a transit center for their troops.

On August 23, Osborne told me that, according to reliable sources, the Germans were most likely to take over Rome and possibly the Vatican City within the next few days. At Osborne's request, my sons used the fireplace in our living room, the only one available to diplomats in the Vatican, to burn the British Legation's confidential documents. But the Germans made no moves during the next few weeks. On September 9, the day before the Germans occupied Rome, I decided that I had better destroy all of my official documents except my accounts, including the two nonconfidential code books, Brown and Gray. My sons proceeded to burn these documents as well in our fireplace.

The Allies and the Badoglio government announced the signing of the Armistice between them on September 8. The Germans in and around Rome, taken by surprise and naturally furious, immediately started to attack Rome. Despite sporadic instances of bravery in resisting the Germans, the leaderless Italian armed forces disintegrated during the following 48 hours. Most of the military donned civilian clothes and went home. The surrender was finally signed in Rome at noon on Friday, September 10. I observed a German artillery bombardment of the Piazza di Spagna area in central Rome from the Papal Palace, which resulted in much smoke and dust, but apparently little damage.

The armistice, followed by the flight of the King and the Badoglio government to Allied-occupied southern Italy, and the takeover of Rome by the German Army, meant that there was no possibility for my brother and me to return to our school in Switzerland. Even if the political situation would have permitted such a trip, I doubt if my mother would ever have allowed us to take another train passing through Italian cities subjected to ever more violent air attacks. So we resigned ourselves to stay in the Vatican until the liberation of Rome by the Allies, which we then thought would happen soon; in fact, we had to wait for nearly nine months. The prospect of a prolonged stay in the Vatican naturally did not please us, as there was little for us to do as young boys. At the ages of eleven and fourteen, we were not particularly interested in exploring the art treasures of the Vatican museum. Our sports activites were limited to occasional tennis games and bicycling in the Vatican gardens. The only other children of our age were the sons of the Bolivian and Venezuelan ambassadors. One useful occupation for me was learning to drive my parents' automobile in the convenient and safe environment of the Vatican gardens.

There was no school in the Vatican, so my parents organized some tutoring lessons for my brother Barclay and me, which usually took place in a room at the Vatican Radio Station put at our disposal by the French speaker, the Belgian Jesuit Father Mistiaen. Mistiaen gave us Latin lessons, while Father Ambord, a Swiss-German Jesuit, taught me German. We studied mathematics with a young Italian engineer, and history and ancient Greek with a Mr. Ivanov, a Russian emigre of French nationality living in Rome. Ivanov did not wish it to be known that he was providing services to Americans, so we would meet him clandestinely at the apartment of a French priest, Monsignor Fontenelle, in the Canonica building next to Santa Marta. But the atmosphere was not particularly conducive to studying, and we practically lost one year of schooling, hopefully compensated by the unique experience we were going through. On weekdays, we normally had two hours of lessons in the morning, followed by a walk in the gardens and lunch with our parents. The afternoons were devoted to homework and reading until teatime in the living room (often with a guest), after which we would play some tennis or bicycle in the Vatican gardens. After dinner, D'Arcy Osborne often joined us and we would discuss the progress of the war until bedtime. It was a relatively comfortable life, as my parents had four servants. But the food situation deteriorated rapidly as 1943 drew to a close, and while we never went hungry, the menus became spartan: little meat and no sweets.

On September 10, Maglione, stating that the situation of the Vatican had become "serious," recommended to the Brazilian

Ambassador, who was the dean of the diplomatic corps, that he warn his colleagues to take precautionary measures regarding their archives in the event that the Germans entered the Vatican City, a move which Maglione said was not entirely to be excluded.

A similar fear had arisen in February, when the Department of State advised me that, according to intelligence sources in Stockholm, one aim of a visit to Rome by Heinrich Himmler in October 1942 was to pressure the Vatican, through the Italian Government, to expel the Allied diplomatic missions, which he described as a "nest of spies," and that instructions to that end were given to the Italian Ambassador to the Holy See, Guariglia. However, Guariglia objected so strenuously that Mussolini rescinded the order. I discussed this report with Cardinal Maglione, who seemed much interested, but refused to confirm or deny the story, although he intimated that the Italian Government had at one time contacted him about expelling the Allied missions. Maglione had refused to consider such a move, pointing out that the presence in the Vatican of the Allied diplomats was the result of the Italian Government's own suggestion. The Cardinal had assured me that it was no longer likely that we should be asked to leave, explaining that the notable increase in the surveillance of diplomats' movements by the Vatican police was due to the exuberance of several of our Latin American colleagues who had been taking Vatican security regulations concerning them too lightly.

At a meeting on September 14, the Allied diplomats decided to follow the Cardinal's advice by destroying all documents that might possibly be of use to the enemy. Osborne and I had already finished our burning, and the others completed theirs without exception by September 23, when I reported to the State Department that my files had been destroyed along with those of the other diplomats.

The Allied diplomats also decided at this time that they

would follow the Holy Father, were he to be forcibly removed to Germany. However, the anxiety of the Vatican progressively abated, as the Germans realized they would have more to lose by removing the Pope than by allowing him to remain, even though he might fall eventually under the exclusive control of the Allies. For the time being, the only danger was a sudden outburst of anger against the Church by Hitler himself, who might overrule the wiser counsels of those who had the long-term interests of Germany at heart. Thus far, the Germans had treated the Holy See with consideration, contributing to the feeling of relative security. The German military commander in Rome posted sentries at the entrance to St. Peter's Square, the boundary line of the Vatican City State.

On September 11, an Italian military government was established in Rome headed by General Calvi di Bergolo, the King's son-in-law, the King and Badoglio having fled to Allied-controlled southern Italy. But when Mussolini, after his liberation by a German commando unit, established a new Fascist government (never recognized by the Holy See) at Salo in northern Italy on September 23, Calvi di Bergolo was arrested and carried off to Germany. The Germans dissolved the Italian military government and assumed control of Rome, with the occasional help of a few remaining Fascists.

One consequence of the disintegration of the Italian armed forces was the release by their Italian guards of thousands of Allied prisoners of war, mostly British. Many of those who had been interned in central Italy headed for Rome, as they believed it would be easier in a large city to hide from the Germans and await the arrival of the Allied armies. A small number managed to sneak into the Vatican City, where they were granted asylum by the Pope and housed in a dormitory in the Papal Gendarmerie barracks. But the Vatican, in order to preserve its neutrality, did its best to prevent Allied prisoners of war from entering the Holy City.

The first three escaped prisoners entered the Vatican on September 10: a Scottish major, a Canadian captain, and a Royal Navy lieutenant. The first two were captured during the Sicilian campaign, while the naval officer was picked up after his submarine had been sunk. My brother and I spent many hours talking to the men, fascinated by their stories about the North African and Sicilian campaigns.

Four days later, two more Royal Navy men entered the Vatican, but this time it was not so easy. Evidently the Vatican authorities worried that they might be facing an unmanageable influx of escapees, and the Vatican gendarmes forced the two men out of St. Peter's and into the square. Hugh Montgomery, Osborne's assistant, arrived on the scene and escorted the two prisoners to the Gate of the Bells, controlled by the Swiss Guards. By this time, the commandant of the Swiss Guards, Colonel de Pfyffer d'Altishofen, had also arrived on the scene; he refused to let the two men enter the Vatican, whereupon Montgomery, an excitable man, accused de Pfyffer of being pro-German. Osborne then intervened, and the Englishmen were allowed to remain in St. Peter's. Shortly thereafter the Vatican agreed to grant them asylum. They turned out to be Navy divers who were caught in Tripoli harbor after a failed attempt to sink an Italian ship by attaching a bomb to its bottom.

By the end of 1943, a few more escaped prisoners managed to enter the Vatican. But outside in Rome, several thousand British and several hundred American escapees were attempting to hide from the Germans to avoid recapture. In a speech he made to the National War College in 1948, my father described how Osborne and he organized assistance for the prisoners:

Disregarding his obligation to respect the neutrality of the Holy See, my British colleague unblushingly set up a clandestine welfare organization for the purpose of catering to the needs of some four thousand British escaped prisoners of war who were hiding from the Germans in various parts of Italy under German occupation. The headquarters of this organization was located in the British Minister's apartment on the top floor of Santa Marta main building. The operations chief was a British infantry major who had been smuggled in for that purpose. He was aided by six or seven "leg men" who traveled widely and supplied the prisoners with food, clothing, medical aid and, above all, money. I had some 230 American escaped prisoners of war in constant touch with me through my own underground and at first I was sending them the necessary supplies through my own channels. However, it gradually became apparent that it was simpler and more economical to use the efficient and much larger British organization for our prisoners as well. So for the last four or five months of the German occupation, the British organization was kind enough to serve the relatively few men that we had along with theirs. All that was necessary for me to do was to supply the cash which I was always able to produce.

A charismatic Irish priest, Monsignor O'Flaherty, was instrumental in setting up and operating the British organization. It was he who smuggled into the Vatican the British major, whose name was Sam Derry, dressed as a priest. O'Flaherty was Derry's chief "leg man" until he received secret warnings that he was due to be arrested by the Germans. He nevertheless continued his work from within the Vatican. O'Flaherty came to dinner with us on several occasions in Santa Marta. I vividly recall his imposing presence (he was a very tall man) and his remarkable sense of humor. He talked freely about his activities on behalf of the escapees, and when he mentioned that in addition to food and lodging, he provided them with weapons, I asked him, half seriously, to bring me a pistol the next time he visited us. A week later,

O'Flaherty came to see us and presented me with a .38 caliber Italian Beretta pistol, the most spectacular souvenir of my Vatican days.

My father's chief "leg man," when he was directly looking after the American escapees, was an American priest attached to the Vatican, Father Joseph McGeogh. According to my father's dispatches to the State Department in late 1943 and early 1944, the equivalent of nearly $9,000 in U.S. Government funds were disbursed through McGeogh and O'Flaherty to aid the American prisoners of war. Both the Vatican and the Germans were undoubtedly aware of the prisoner assistance efforts emanating from the British and U.S. diplomatic missions, which were obviously in violation of the Vatican's neutrality. In any event, the Vatican chose to turn a blind eye on the activity, possibly because it could be regarded as charitable aid to destitute prisoners. Presumably the Vatican was unaware of O'Flaherty's involvement with weapons.

My father was also involved in helping Jewish refugees in Italy. In corresponding after his retirement with Jacques de Blesson, the Counselor of the French Embassy during the war years in the Vatican, my father recalled the providing of financial help by himself and D'Arcy Osborne for such refugees in Italy through counterpart funds deposited in a New York bank. The "leg man" between them and the Jewish organization in Rome was a French Canon of St. Peter's, Monsignor Herissé. We would often see him going in and out of Santa Marta, where he lived. A spry, white-haired little man with a sharp wit, he did not hide his complete support for the Allied cause. We ran into him one day in the courtyard of Santa Marta and chatted with him about current war developments. One piece of news we brought up was the sinking of a German troopship by a British submarine, resulting in the deaths of several hundred German soldiers. Herissé, in an un-Christianlike outburst, said: "Pas assez! (Not enough!)" Herissé and another pro-Allied French priest, Monsignor Fontenelle, were particularly active in clandestine operations.

Another event during the closing months of 1943 provided us with some additional, and unwanted, excitement. At around 8 P.M. on November 5, as we were playing our customary family game of bridge, a huge explosion shook our apartment. Since a small plane had been circling overhead for the past hour, we guessed that bombs had been dropped. My first reaction was to rush under our heavy dining room table, which would provide some protection from falling debris, where I bumped heads with our butler, who had the same idea. But as our apartment seemed intact and no further explosions occurred, we went down to the Santa Marta courtyard, where a small crowd of excited diplomats and nuns had gathered. The assumption was that bombs must have fallen in Rome near the Vatican. Barclay had disappeared during this time, but he soon returned and breathlessly told us that the bombs had exploded within the Vatican City. Walking toward the Vatican gardens, we could make out several craters, but it was too dark to see exactly what had been hit. The ground was covered with mud, broken glass, and other debris.

The next day we saw that four bombs had exploded inside the Vatican. The Vatican administration building (Governatorato) suffered considerable damage, as did the mosaic factory. The Bernini stained glass windows in St. Peter's were broken in many places; the basilica was closed for several days for repairs. By a stroke of luck, none of the bombs hit an inhabited building and no one was killed or wounded. Our apartment was not harmed, as it was shielded from the blasts by the main Santa Marta building, where many windowpanes were broken. Perhaps our main worry when we saw the damage to the Governatorato building was the fate of our food supplies, which were stored there. But they were intact, except for a few broken wine bottles.

Cardinal Maglione promptly asked the U.S., British, and German governments to investigate the incident, and again insisted that all pilots be given strict instructions not to overfly the Vatican City. The State Department issued a report on November 9 declaring that no Allied planes had flown over Rome the evening of November 5, although a number of British planes had carried out raids in the vicinity of the capital at that time. A week later, the Apostolic Delegate in Washington informed the State Department that the bombs that fell on the Vatican weighed between 100 and 150 kilograms, set for immediate explosion, leaving only small craters but causing extensive damage over a large surface area. The bomb fragments collected by the Vatican authorities did not lead to any conclusions as to their origin. The identity of the airplane that bombed the Vatican has remained a mystery, although the most likely theory is that the bombs were jettisoned by a British aircraft in distress.

A small plane had been heard flying over Rome and the Vatican for over an hour prior to the attack, and the diplomats speculated that it might have dropped the bombs, as a provocation by either the Germans or the Italian fascists. The bombing was unnerving for the residents of the Vatican, who had previously considered themselves immune from such attacks. Our anxiety increased as the lone, single-engine plane reappeared on clear nights, flying low over Rome and over the Vatican itself. It came to be known as la vedova nera (the black widow). In the weeks following the bombing, we would head for the basement of the main Santa Marta building when we heard the sound of the "black widow," but soon decided that it was not worth the trouble.

On December 8, Under-Secretary of State Stettinius informed the Apostolic Delegate in Washington that General Eisenhower had given instructions to the crews of aircraft under his command not to fly over the Vatican City, which was to be respected as a neutral state. The Vatican nevertheless sent several notices to my father and to the State Department, in December 1943 and especially in the first months of 1944, that Allied planes had violated Vatican airspace contrary to Eisenhower's instructions. However, perhaps recognizing that overflights of an area as tiny as the Vatican City were inevitable, the Holy See did not demand further action by the Allied high command.

On December 1, I reported that the Vatican now viewed the idea of Rome as an open city as purely a military question, meaning that steps should be taken to prevent Rome from becoming a battlefield either through agreement between belligerent parties or through Allied strategy. In practice, this meant that before the arrival of the Allies in Rome, the Germans would have to withdraw.

By December 1943, the Holy See appeared to be satisfied with the treatment it had received from the German authorities in Rome. There were signs of increasing German warmth toward the Vatican, for which there was no adequate explanation. The Germans were also ingratiating themselves with the Roman population by liquidating local Fascist organizations, which had become obnoxious. As a result, the Germans remained the only authorities exercising effective power in Rome.

After the Germans took over Rome on September 10, 1943, air-raid alarms regularly sounded by day and night. However, with the exception of the air attack on the Vatican City on November 5, 1943, no bombs of any size were dropped inside the Rome area up to the end of the year. On the other hand, the environs of Rome and the nearby airfields were continually bombed by the Allies, which explained the continued alarms in Rome itself. Every night when the weather was good, the sky was filled with bursts of anti-aircraft fire and red and white flares dropped from the planes. From time to time at night a small German plane would drop a bomb or two in the middle of the city itself, apparently as reprisals on individuals, since the targets seemed to be carefully sought out. Since accurate identification was not possible at night, the offending plane might have been Fascist Republican rather than German.

The Combined Chiefs of Staff in Washington informed Eisenhower's headquarters in Algiers on December 15 that (1) the Vatican City should be treated as an independent neutral state entitled to normal rights of a neutral; (2) the Allied Forces must take every precaution to avoid violating the territory of the Vatican City as defined by the Lateran Treaty; (3) Allied troops must also avoid a number of other churches and buildings in Rome which were situated outside the Vatican City, but were the property of the Holy See. These properties were defined in the Lateran Treaty and had full diplomatic immunity. However, the message pointed out that "the diplomatic immunity of Vatican properties located in Rome should not be allowed to interfere with military operations, artillery fire, bombing etc., during the assault."

At the end of 1943, my father began reporting on the political and social situation in German-occupied Italy. Following the Armistice of September 8, the King and Marshal Badoglio continued to act as the established government of Italy, with the consent of the Allies. In Rome, members of various non-Fascist political groups created an underground "Committee for National Liberation" to prepare for a democratic government following the end of the war. The Committee was presided over by Ivanoe Bonomi. Six parties were involved: three moderate pro-Monarchy groups—Liberals, Christian Democrats, and Labor Democrats—and three radical left-wing groups— Socialists, Communists, and Party of Action. A member of the Committee, whom my father does not identify, prepared for him a memorandum describing the committee's composition and activities as of December 1, 1943. In forwarding the memorandum to Robert Murphy, the State Department's political adviser on Eisenhower's staff, my father wrote that since the leaders of the parties had to remain more or less in hiding, little progress had been made by the Committee other than passing a resolution calling for the establishment of an anti-Fascist government of transition following the liberation of Rome. He concluded pessimistically:

The situation of German-occupied Italy is appalling. The people have no one to guide them, no program on which to base hopes for the future, no principles to fight for, no confidence in themselves. Great numbers of young men are in hiding, hoping thus to escape enrolment in the German or Fascist armies, or deportation as workers to Germany, but in my judgment it seems at least questionable whether many of them would not make equally strenuous efforts when the time comes to avoid fighting or working for the Allies. The people feel that their material assets have either already been completely wiped out or will be in the near future if the war continues as at present. The military collapse of the Italian army when faced by the Germans last September, together with the political confusion surrounding the Armistice dealt them a moral blow from which they show no signs yet of recovery. As a result of this moral bankruptcy, the more ugly sides of the Italian nature, such as the practice of delation, are being revealed from time to time, but such manifestations are happily counterbalanced by the nobility of spirit displayed by the population throughout the land, especially the peasants, in granting hospitality at great personal risk to our destitute ex-prisoners of war. There must of course be other bright spots in the foregoing gloomy picture. Men of courage who are doing fine jobs do exist. But from all I can learn, they are too few to affect appreciably the general situation. The conclusion seems inescapable that the great majority of Italians, at least in German-occupied Italy, have for the time being fallen into such a state of inertia and despair that they are looking to any agency rather than their own will-power for salvation. They would prefer by far that the agency should be the Allies.

In a telegram dated December 16, my father expressed the same pessimistic views of the Italian situation:

While realizing that according to the Moscow Three-Power Declaration on Italy it is considered essential by us that the present [Badoglio] Italian Government be made more democratic, I nevertheless venture to point out that the vast majority of the Italian people—at least in areas occupied by the Germans—are completely indifferent to questions of domestic government at the present stage, since they have far more pressing demands on their attention. To judge the state of mind of a large section of the population, it should be remembered that according to all reports the Germans are leaving a veritable desert behind them as they move northward. Refugees from the battlefront who have lost literally everything are settling temporarily in centers further up the peninsula where the recital of their harrowing experiences is causing consternation among the populations in these centers who realize that in their turn they may soon undergo the same fate. The major preoccupation not only of refugees but of the ordinary citizen today is food, clothing and shelter, in short, physical security. Under these circumstances, even for a politically minded people, which the Italians are not, solicitude in making their government more democratic would seem to be out of the question. There are many who feel therefore that in the interests of democracy itself it would be the wiser course to postpone agitation in domestic politics until a more propitious moment, rather than to continue efforts to have a few politicians working in a vacuum decide questions which should be the concern of the whole people. I understand that the Rome Committee itself would be willing to lay such questions aside until after the end of hostilities and to carry on until then with the present set up of the Italian [Royalist] Government. The Italian people themselves, I feel confident, would ask for nothing better than to be governed by the Allies for a long period to come.

In the final days of 1943, my father had his customary end-of-the-year audience with the Pope:

The Holy Father's chief preoccupation was his fear of Communism. He also expressed apprehension lest the departure of General Eisenhower from the Mediterranean Theater and his replacement by a British general might mean less consideration in the future for the Vatican by the Allied High Command. I felt at the time that this fear reflected the Vatican belief that an anti-Catholic strain ran through the British Government, due chiefly to the presence of Eden. I assured His Holiness that operations in Italy had been a joint Anglo-American enterprise, and that I had received no indication that any change was contemplated.

On December 24, 1943, the Pope celebrated the traditional Christmas midnight mass in his private chapel, attended by the entire diplomatic corps—Allied, Axis and neutral. This time, however, the mass took place at 5 P.M. because the curfew in effect in Rome would have made it impossible for the diplomats residing outside the Vatican to attend. While the ceremony retained its dramatic character because of the close proximity of diplomats from enemy countries in the intimacy of the Matilda Chapel as the Holy Father celebrated the mass, the early hour greatly reduced its impact. After the mass was over, we walked back to our Santa Marta quarters for a family Christmas dinner. But the traditional holiday cheer was absent. The severe wartime rationing limited us to a Spartan meal, and we had only a few improvised Christmas decorations. We could not help wondering how much longer our "imprisonment" in the Vatican would last, and as 1943 drew to a close, the mood was pessimistic. The Allied armies seemed to be bogged down in front of the German Gustav line of defense north of Naples, and repeated attacks in the

Cassino area were unsuccessful. We wondered whether this Christmas would really be the last one we would spend inside the Vatican, as we had hoped and expected when the Allies landed on the Italian peninsula earlier in the year.

CHAPTER 5

1944

*A*lthough there was a stalemate on the ground, Allied air attacks were steadily increasing in frequency and intensity in the early days of 1944. Not unexpectedly, the raids continued to cause civilian casualties among the Italian population, as well as destruction of, and damage to, church property. As a result, my father's dealings with the Vatican authorities during the first five months of 1944 were almost exclusively related to Allied air activity, as the Holy See tried desperately to persuade the British and American governments to spare the Vatican, Rome, and papal property elsewhere in Italy.

A major concern for the Vatican was the preservation of the Papal Domain of Castel Gandolfo, located in the Alban Hills south of Rome. The extensive property, which was considered neutral Vatican territory, contained a villa that the popes in peacetime had used as their summer residence. In August 1943, my father forwarded to Myron Taylor in Washington, at the request of the Vatican, a detailed description of the property, including a map, in order that steps be taken to avoid the bombing of Castel Gandolfo. This information was apparently transmitted to the War Department.

On January 23, 1944, Allied forces established a beachhead at Anzio, some thirty miles south of Rome, with the aim of outflanking the Gustav Line. When we heard the news, we had high hopes that the liberation of Rome was imminent, but once again we would be disappointed, as the Germans effectively contained this threat. The newly *landed British and American troops were subjected to deadly artillery fire from German guns emplaced in the Alban Hills overlooking the beachhead. Although Castel Gandolfo was located in a part of the hills that did not face Anzio, it was disturbingly close to the front, and it was perhaps inevitable that bombs would fall on the Papal Domain. During the first half of February, Allied planes bombed Castel Gandolfo at least four times, causing much damage and killing hundreds of the 15,000 refugees whom the Vatican was sheltering on its property. The Vatican protested these raids to the British and American governments, but the Allied High Command claimed that the Papal Domain was "saturated with Germans." Asserting first-hand knowledge, the Vatican rejected the Allied claim and stated that no German soldier had ever entered the Papal Domain. In fact, German policy was scrupulously to respect the neutrality of Vatican properties; the German Embassy had informed the Holy See that Field Marshall Kesselring had issued instructions forbidding the use of Castel Gandolfo and its immediate vicinity for military purposes. My father wrote:*

While the Vatican expressed some annoyance with the Allied statement that Castel Gandolfo was "saturated with Germans," I felt that it showed surprising forbearance when discussing with me the tragedies that occurred in that area as a result of Allied bombings. The Vatican apparently realized that mischances were inevitable in warfare. However, results of bombings did not appear to have been effective against [the] Germans, creating a bad impression among the Italians. Commendatore Bonomelli, the manager of the Papal Domain, said that he was sickened at the sight of so many dead bodies, but he had yet to see one dead German. It would seem, in fact, that German soldiers had an uncanny way of disappearing into thin air at the approach of hostile aircraft, and reappearing immediately after the raid in order to crowd the roads again.

As a consequence of the air attacks on Castel Gandolfo, the Vatican relocated the refugees to Vatican institutions within the city of Rome, transporting as well forty cows into the Vatican City, where they were housed in a storage area under the Vatican Museum.

On February 17, American bombers totally destroyed the Monastery of Monte Cassino, the Allies asserting, without proof, that the monastery was occupied by the German Army. My father had to face the anger of the Vatican authorities. In a dispatch to the State Department dated February 19, he wrote:

Re bombing of Monte Cassino by Allies. Vatican is outwardly assuming a noncommital attitude . . . It is evident, however, high Vatican officials are holding Allies responsible. Cardinal Maglione spoke to me about the matter this morning with some heat. He said that he was convinced from evidence at hand there were no German soldiers, gun emplacements, etc., in Monastery or immediate neighborhood, although he admitted he was unable to specify exactly extent of "immediate neighborhood." He added he thought the bombing entirely unnecessary from a military point of view, was a "collossal blunder" and a "piece of gross stupidity" on the part of Allies because needless destruction of this symbol of civilization was bound to react unfavorably on pro-Ally opinion everywhere. I told the Cardinal I did not believe for a minute the Allies would have destroyed Monastery had there not been overriding military reasons and I did not think he was justified in being so positive since only those on the spot were in a position to pass definitive judgment. To this he replied, "Pardon me if I say so, but I know what I am talking about and have access to sources of information that are probably not open to you." I was forced to admit that my only source so far was the radio.

Maglione said German Ambassador had suggested that

Holy See issue a public statement deploring the incident but that he had refused "at least so far" on grounds that Holy See did not wish to become involved in a controversy between belligerent parties. The Cardinal hinted, however, that Holy See might feel obliged to make some sort of public statement later on after further investigation. I said I thought any finger pointing at this late date in war would be badly received in general and especially in countries whose monuments had been destroyed by Germans. It is likely, however, that Holy See, having openly championed the cause of Monte Cassino and being convinced of German good faith in present instance, will find it difficult to remain silent, especially under German pressure.

In subsequent communications to the U.S. government, the Vatican noted that the abbey of Monte Cassino was "falsely described as a German fortress." In early April, my father informed Tardini that the Allied commanders had unquestionable evidence that the Abbey of Monte Cassino formed part of the German defense system. This provoked, for the first time, an official memorandum from the Vatican Secretariat of State on the subject of Monte Cassino. The memorandum stated that despite the views of the Allied commanders on the subject, the Holy See could only repeat what it had originally told my father, namely that the abbot and a few monks remained in the monastery until the last moment, to make sure that nothing would compromise the safety of the monastery, and have given written assurances to the Vatican that no German soldiers or military equipment were ever inside the monastery. Nevertheless, the American Government continued to assert the contrary.

In early 1944, there was a notable increase in American bombing attacks on the Rome area, although, as before, the historical center of the city was spared. Principal targets continued to be airfields and railroad facilities, but the raids resulted in hundreds of civilian casu-

alties and much civilian property damage; several districts were without water. The Vatican, mainly through the Apostolic Delegate in Washington, continued to object to the bombings, pointing out that on a number of occasions, no military purpose could be attributed to the raids. This was particularly true of bombings on March 14 and March 18, which caused much damage to residential areas, including several hospitals and churches, without hitting any military installations. Through his contacts in Rome, my father was convinced that the military value of these particular raids was negligible, and that they were fueling anti-Allied sentiments among the Romans. He reported these views to the State Department in a dispatch dated March 25:

Many civilian lives were lost when bombs were dropped during [the raids of March 14 and March 18] in residential districts. From all reports military effects were negligible, especially in March 18 raid, when only two bombs fell within the enclosure of Macao Barracks, which apparently was main target. This last raid was carried out by waves of medium or light bombers between 3 and 4 o'clock in afternoon when population accustomed to morning intrusions was not expecting it and latter circumstance may have had something to do with large number of casualties . . . While it is of course impossible for me to pass judgment on military value of such raids, I do feel it my duty even at risk of repetition to report that in opinion of our best friends here [a reference to my father's numerous pro-Ally Italian friends in Rome] moral damage done to our cause far outweighs possible military advantages. These friends insist raids of this nature in which people are unable to perceive any military gain for Allies in compensation for their sufferings have to a large extent already turned public opinion against us and thus have played squarely into hands of our enemies . . . While much of pessimism in foregoing picture is undoubtedly well founded, I nevertheless feel confident once Allies are here spirits will rise again and past disappointments will be forgotten.

A few weeks prior to this message, my father had taken a different position concerning a raid that took place on March 3. He reported to the State Department on March 6:

Vatican high officials as usual seem considerably upset by Allied daylight raid March 3, which they maintain was made on Rome although objectives obviously restricted to railway yards and other military targets in periphery of city. Unfortunately, according to a Vatican report, some 500 civilians were killed, but it seems largest proportion of this loss due to mischance when shelter received direct hit. Resentment of air attacks in Rome area has become so fixed an idea with Vatican that any recognition of the good work (of which I am told there is ample evidence in present instance) accomplished by our airmen seems to be precluded. Two articles in *Osservatore Romano* [the Vatican newspaper] are misleading in that they give the impression only civilian damage done. I have taken occasion to protest to appropriate authorities against this one-sided method of presenting the facts.

Despite the human tragedies associated with the bombing of the Rome area, the air raids broke the monotony of our daily life inside the Vatican and often provided us with some spectacular sights. On January 13, as I was coming out of the Vatican Radio Station at noon following my lessons, I heard the sound of many motors. Looking up, I saw formations of American bombers over Rome, escorted by twin-tailed Lockheed Lightning fighters flying directly over the Vatican. The Lightnings were then attacked by German fighter planes, and I witnessed a number of dogfights, with clearly audible machine-gun firing. I heard something strike the soil near me, and later learned that several cannon shells had exploded within the Vatican, fortunately without injuries or damage. As usual on such occasions, members of the diplomatic community, including my mother, gathered on the terrace of the Santa Marta building to view the air raid, and actually witnessed the shooting down of one of the Lightnings. They were relieved to see a parachute floating down in the vicinity of the crashed plane. During a subsequent raid, we saw a large black object spiraling down toward us from a formation of bombers flying overhead. It landed with a loud bang, on a house just outside the walls of the Vatican, and then fell onto the street, after setting fire to the house. We later learned that it was a spare fuel tank jettisoned by one of the American planes.

After the landings at Anzio, we would often hear the distant rumble of gunfire from that direction, and at night the sky over the beachhead would be filled with tiny pinpoints of light, as in a gigantic fireworks display. We were witnessing Allied anti-aircraft barrages, since the Germans had deployed their few remaining aircraft to attack the substantial armada of ships supplying the troops ashore.

Allied prisoners of war continued to trickle into the Vatican, providing us some additional relief from the boredom of our daily routine, including two American airmen who had managed to scale the Vatican walls.

Two unusual escapees appeared on our doorstep at the beginning of February. They were female clerical employees of the U.S. Consulate in Monte Carlo: Mrs. Charrier, a young American woman married to a Frenchman, and Miss Houldon, a middle-aged Englishwoman. Since they were U.S. Foreign Service personnel, my father decided to house them in our apartment. They had been through a harrowing experience before finally finding refuge in the Vatican. In November 1942, the Italians seized the Principality of Monaco, whose neutrality had hitherto been respected. Up to that *time, the U.S. Consulate continued to operate under Consul Walter Orebaugh, for whom Mrs. Charrier and Miss Houlden worked. The Italians arrested Orebaugh and the two secretaries, interning them first in Gubbio, northeast of Florence, and later in Perugia. Following the armistice of September 1943, Orebaugh and the two ladies were set free, with, however, nowhere to go. They found an abandoned house in Perugia where they could hide, remaining there for the next five months, with little food and no heating. Orebaugh eventually decided to try to join Italian partisans, while the women headed for Rome, with the assistance of an Italian who had been helping escaped prisoners of war. They managed to enter the Vatican using false identity cards.*

Since the end of 1943, the food situation in Rome had continuously deteriorated, causing much anxiety in Vatican circles. The Vatican decided to put at the disposal of the Rome municipal authorities a fleet of trucks to bring much needed food to the city from Vatican supplies in northern Italy. The roofs of the Vatican trucks were painted yellow and white—the Vatican colors—and were marked with the words "Vatican State." The Secretariat of State asked my father to notify the Allied commanders of the presence of Vatican motor convoys, with their distinctive markings, on roads leading to Rome from the north of Italy, and requested that they not be attacked by Allied planes. Nevertheless, Vatican trucks were machine-gunned and bombed on a number of occasions, resulting in the deaths of several drivers.

The Vatican protested these attacks, but my father informed the Secretariat of State that, according to the Allied Command, it was virtually impossible for Allied warplanes attacking road transport to distinguish particular markings on motor vehicles. The Vatican authorities were not convinced; Monsignor Montini, at the Pope's suggestion, took my father to the roof of St. Peter to view several Vatican trucks in St. Peter's Square below and thus demonstrate that the trucks were easily recognizable from above. Although agreeing that this was so, my father pointed out that recognition of such trucks from airplanes flying at high speeds was a different matter. He could only repeat that the Allied air forces could not guarantee the immunity of the Vatican truck convoys, even though pilots would be requested to avoid attacking Vatican vehicles to the extent possible. Much to the distress of the Vatican, such attacks continued on a regular basis. My father's notes refer to this message sent from British Air Marshal Slessor to his U.S. counterpart: "Vatican now admits that their convoys are part of a regular service for feeding Rome and in effect they are thus breaking the blockade we are imposing on Rome and are thus performing an unneutral act."

The British view was that not only was immunity for Vatican trucks impossible for tactical reasons, but also undesirable for strategic reasons as well. Slessor's message is curious, as neither my father nor the Vatican ever referred to a "blockade" of Rome by the Allied air forces.

As late as the middle of May, we feared that we would be facing another long, hot summer inside the Vatican City. The Allied armies seemed unable to make any significant progress against the German defenses on the Cassino and Anzio fronts. My diary entry of May 1 noted that "Now the days are getting duller and duller. As the heat gradually increases, we are all getting more tired and depressed." But our mood changed rapidly after the launching of new Allied offensives in the Cassino area on May 12 and from the beachhead on May 23. It soon became clear that the attacks were succeeding and that the German Army was retreating.

To our great relief, it appeared that the Germans were not going to make a stand in Rome. The withdrawing German forces were under constant air attack by American fighter-bombers, which we could observe dive-bombing targets on the outskirts of Rome. During the closing days of May and the first few days of June, we could also see, from the top of the Vatican gardens, huge columns of smoke on the Alban Hills, as well as bursting artillery shells.

By June 3, Allied troops were on the outskirts of Rome. My father recalled that day in his notes:

There were especially good vantage points along the walls of the Vatican gardens to view the expanse of country outside Rome in every direction. We took advantage of this during the approach of the Allied armies. I remember vividly that in the late afternoon of June 3, we could see that a tank battle was in progress near Lanuvio in the plains below the Alban Hills. A great cloud of smoke and dust hung over the battlefield, so that it was difficult to make out the details of what was actually going on. Every once in a while, perhaps every ten minutes, a tank would lumber out of the cloud into the open, followed by another, both firing at each other at a great rate. After a few minutes both tanks would return to the melee inside the cloud. One could hear at all times the continual roar of the guns. It was an unusual experience to be a witness of such slaughter from the gardens of the Prince of Peace on Earth.

We did not sleep well during the night of June 3, because of the noise generated by the retreating German troops. One of the main roads to the north of Rome, the Via Aurelia, passed by the Vatican walls close to Santa Marta. Because of the Allied air attacks, the Germans moved their heavy equipment primarily by night. Some German vehicles would take a wrong turn up a dead-end street not far from us, resulting in much shouting and grinding of gears. Unable to sleep, I went to the roof of the main Santa Marta building to view the German trucks and tanks moving north.

We spent the next day watching the retreating German Army, as I noted in my diary:

I had the best view of all, as I had gone into the nuns' gar-
den which overlooks the road on which the Germans were
retreating. I brought my camera and took many pictures. It
was very interesting. One could tell that the Germans were
lacking motor transport, for they were extensively using
horses to draw wagons and every kind of contraption you
could think of. Some were even on bicycles. They had stolen
all Rome's horsedrawn cabs [no doubt a fifteen-year-old's
exaggeration]. They also used horses to pull their artillery.
One felt rather sorry for them; they looked so young. Some
were tired and dirty, but others looked perfectly fit. Not all
Germans had managed to steal a horse or a bicycle, for there
were long columns of them marching. Those were the ones
that really looked exhausted. Some had to carry machine guns
on their shoulders. They looked terribly depressed. Some
stopped right below me and sat down on some grass. Others
bought some filthy lemonade from a little stand, also right
below me. I must say that the Romans were very kind to
them, although they were immensely relieved to see them
leaving. They gave the Germans drinks and cigarettes. It is in
the character of Romans to be kind to everyone in trouble.

This stream of Germans continued intermittently all dur-
ing the day. Towards 5 P.M. I went up on the terrace [of the
Santa Marta building]. It was very crowded, because all the
South Americans had come up there to watch the Germans.
Now there were many more Germans on foot. Many were
limping. Sometimes groups of these Germans would sit down
on the curb and wait for trucks to pick them up. We watched
this until 6 P.M. Then began the dive bombing. Dozens of our
planes came over and started bombing the Germans just out-
side of Rome, near enough for us to see the bombs falling out
of the planes. We could also see the little spurts of flame on

their wings as they began machine gunning the road. It was rather sickening to see tired German boys walking past us and then watch them dive-bombed and strafed. The dive-bombing lasted at least an hour.

Early the next morning, June 5, our entire family went to the spot in the nuns' garden where I had been watching the Germans the previous day, and joyfully witnessed the passage of American army vehicles heading north in pursuit of the Germans. A Jeep stopped briefly below us, and we shouted welcoming words in English to its occupants. Obviously surprised, one of the soldiers asked us who we were. When he learned that we were Americans, he reached in the back of the vehicle, pulled out a carton of cigarettes, a box of Hershey bars, and a copy of Time magazine, which he proceeded to toss over the wall in our direction. This was our first, happy contact with American soldiers.

Rome was liberated by American and British troops with scarcely any fighting taking place within the city itself. Although Rome was never officially recognized by the Allies as an "open city," it was as a practical matter treated as such by the belligerents. The German Army destroyed none of the bridges crossing the Tiber to delay the pursuing Allied troops, and the Allies refrained from bombing them, which could have trapped German forces on the south side of the river. It is surely fair to assume that the continuous appeals of the Holy See to both sides must have contributed to sparing Rome from the destruction that would have ensued had the city become a battlefield. The Romans were of course immensely relieved by their relatively painless liberation, for which they seemed to give credit to the Pope. On June 5, the first day of the liberation of Rome, a huge crowd of cheering Romans filled St. Peter's Square, where they were blessed by the Holy Father.

During the next few days, we took full advantage of our newly *found freedom to drive all over Rome, which was swarming with American and British troops. My father was besieged by American VIPs who wanted to meet the Pope, and spent much time arranging audiences for such dignitaries as General Mark Clark, commander of the 5th U.S. Army, and General Eisenhower. One of our first visitors was a cousin of my mother, Colonel Robert Dulaney, commanding a regiment of the 45th Infantry Division. To the great excitement of my brother Barclay and myself, he invited both of us to spend a night at his regimental headquarters some fifteen miles north of Rome, and we thus had the chance to experience a wartime army bivouac. We were not in danger, as the Germans had retreated far to the north. We were picked up the next day by my mother, who somehow managed to find her way through the heavy military traffic on the Via Aurelia.*

The most urgent problem facing my father following the liberation of Rome was to find a suitable lodging in Rome, for the Vatican was pressing the Allied diplomats to move out of the Vatican City. The members of the Axis embassies to the Holy See remained in Rome after the departure of the German forces, and were placed in protective custody by the Allied forces. The Holy See wanted to receive them within the Vatican, which was an impossibility without the prior departure of the Allied diplomats. Myron Taylor, who arrived in Rome in the middle of June, was anxious to accommodate the Vatican in this respect, and ordered my father to move out of Santa Marta as soon as possible. My father finally found a large apartment in the center of Rome with a splendid view of the Ara Coeli Church and Piazza Venezia, and we moved out of Santa Marta on July 8. Our former Vatican home was turned over to the Japanese diplomats. The British Minister and some of the South Americans took much longer to move out, to the great annoyance of the Vatican authorities. In fact, the British Government first disputed the obligation to move their representative out to make place for enemy diplomats, but changed its mind when the Americans sensibly complied with the Vatican request. Besides the German and Japanese embassies, the Romanian, Slovakian, Hungarian, and Finnish diplomats accredited to the Holy See also moved into the Vatican City in July 1944.

Myron Taylor settled down in an elegant town house near the Spanish Steps, the American Embassy providing office space for his mission in its annex on Via Boncompagni. Taylor actually spent little time on Vatican affairs, as he was primarily involved with Italian relief programs. My father remained in Rome as Myron Taylor's assistant (the title of chargé d'affaires would no longer apply, since Taylor was present in Rome) until the first half of 1946, when he was appointed ambassador to Haiti by President Truman. The Taylor mission lasted until 1949, Truman having in turn named Taylor as his personal representative to the Pope. My father's memoirs ended with his move out of the Vatican in July 1944, but it is appropriate to conclude the story of his Vatican assignment by reproducing a memorandum he wrote to Myron Taylor on June 4, 1945, reporting on a conversation with Dr. Josef Mueller, a Bavarian Catholic lawyer who had been a leading figure in the anti-Nazi German underground movement and had acted as the liaison between that movement and the Holy See. My father met Mueller following a speech by the Pope to the College of Cardinals on June 2, 1945, during which the Pope had severely castigated National Socialism and had referred to the deaths of 2000 Catholic priests at Dachau.

<u>FOR THE AMBASSADOR</u>   June 4, 1945

   Dr. Mueller told me last night that contrary to what I had heard, he had no part in drafting any part of the Pope's speech, but that he had furnished the Holy Father with the information on which certain passages were based.

Dr. Mueller said that during the war his anti-Nazi organization in Germany had always been very insistent that the Pope should refrain from making any public statement singling out the Nazis and specifically condemning them and had recommended that the Pope's remarks should be confined to generalities only. Dr. Mueller said that he was obliged to give this advice, since, if the Pope had been specific, Germans would have accused him of yielding to the promptings of foreign powers and this would have made the German Catholics even more suspected than they were and would have greatly restricted their freedom of action in their work of resistance to the Nazis. Dr. Mueller said that the policy of the Catholic resistance in Germany was that the Pope should stand aside while the German hierarchy carried out the struggle against the Nazis inside Germany, without outside influence being brought to bear. Dr. Mueller said that the Pope had followed this advice throughout the war.

I then said to Dr. Mueller that I had heard rather widespread criticism of the Pope in connection with his latest speech, because he had waited until Germany had been defeated before attacking the Nazis in public. Dr. Mueller said that he had already explained why the Pope had maintained silence during the war. He imagined that the Pope had decided to come out in the open now against the Nazis because the implications in the denunciations were so very important at the present time and seemed to the Pope to override other considerations.

H.H.T

Index